To all the Sailors at Mattituck Library

All the Best

Buddy Hedger

SAILING SMART

SAILING SMART

Winning Techniques, Tactics, and Strategies

BUDDY MELGES AND CHARLES MASON

Drawings by Ted Brennan

HENRY HOLT AND COMPANY • NEW YORK

Published by Henry Holt and Company, Inc.,
521 Fifth Avenue, New York, New York 10175.

Published simultaneously in Canada.

Library of Congress Cataloging in Publication Data

Melges, Buddy
Sailing smart.

1. Sailing.   I. Mason, Charles.   II. Title.
VK543.M37   1983   797.1'4   82–15557
ISBN 0-8050-0200-6

Designer: Helene Berinsky
Printed in the United States of America
10 9 8 7 6 5 4 3 2

ISBN 0-8050-0200-6

Where boats are evenly matched in the matter of speed and draught, it is the quality of the piloting that wins the race.

—MARK TWAIN

CONTENTS

ACKNOWLEDGMENTS

Several people have given unsparingly of their time to assist this effort. Lydia Orcutt helped type the original manuscript; Ted Brennan combined his extraordinary artistic skills with his sailor's understanding; and Paul Bresnick of Holt, in addition to handling the stopwatch, recommended some key course changes and kept his experienced hand on the editorial helm throughout. Finally, a special thanks to everyone who has sailed with us and competed against us over the years. You have been perhaps the best teachers of all.

INTRODUCTION

I first met Buddy Melges during his campaign leading up to the 1972 Olympic Trials in San Francisco. Later, I had an opportunity to observe his magnificent sailing skills during the Olympic Games in Kiel, West Germany. Buddy had already become a legend in the United States. But at Kiel he would match his sailing skills against most of the best sailors in the world, including Paul Elvström, the champion sailor from Denmark.

The rest, of course, is history. Buddy and his Soling crew won Olympic gold medals in convincing fashion. (Incidentally, no American sailor has won a gold medal since.) As I watched that Olympic regatta I was struck by two things: Buddy's extraordinary sailing abilities on the water, and the large amount of time and care Buddy spent ashore answering questions put to him by his fellow sailors, journalists, and the general public. All were interested to know how he sailed so well over such a wide range of wind and sea conditions.

Since those Games I have watched Buddy compete in many other regattas. He continues to deliver the same outstanding performances on the race course. And he still gives freely of his time to others interested in learning more about sailing. It is these qualities, both as a competitor and as a sportsman, that have always impressed me.

Buddy continues to bring his talents to new classes of boats. In Stars, for example, he has won two consecutive world championships, the first one coming in his very first year in the class. In the years preceding the 1980 Olympic Trials, Buddy sailed both the Star *and* the Soling at the world-class level—a truly phenomenal achievement.

His enthusiasm for the sport remains unbounded and it is shared equally by his wife, Gloria. They have, in turn, instilled this enthusiasm in their children, Laura, Harry, and Hans, all of whom are excellent sailors in their own right.

Buddy can expound on sailing for hours with precision and great humor. I have listened to him at dinner after a long day of iceboating, while a Wisconsin winter storm began to swirl around the large Victorian house he and Gloria own on the shore of Lake Geneva. We've talked about the sport while we sat on their dock, our backs warmed by a welcome spring sun. And I've discussed sailing with Buddy as we stood motionless at the end of a crisp fall day and watched ducks and geese swooping low over the Wisconsin cornfields as they migrated south.

Buddy is enthusiastic about life in general, but he is particularly happy when he is out of doors. He understands, appreciates, and respects what nature can create—and that, I think, helps explain why he is such a superb sailor. He has a sensitivity to those natural elements around him that adds an extra dimension to his sailing. Though Buddy has been offered the helms of 12-Meters and other large boats, he has always preferred to sail and to compete in small boats—the one-design classes. He knows they are the boats that keep a sailor in touch with the wind and the water.

In sailing, as in any sport, you must have the desire to keep trying to improve your abilities. You have to spend time on the water with your boat and your crew, so you can hear what the boat and the wind are saying. When you believe you honestly know your own capabilities, you are ready to start winning consistently. Winning one race, then losing the next one by a wide margin, doesn't really count. It is consistency over time that should be your goal.

Though sailing does have systems, procedures, and tactics, Buddy always says that it is possible to get too wound up in technical details and to make the mistake of "sailing your bowplate." If you do that, he says, you won't be able to see the bigger picture painted by the boats around you on the race course. He also says that most of the success in sailboat racing comes not from technical breakthroughs but rather from going out on the water and perfecting the basic maneuvers of tacking, gybing, and steering.

If you can combine these fundamentals with a fraction of the dedication and enthusiasm for sailing that Buddy Melges has, you will be well on your way toward achieving your own championship performances.

—CHARLES MASON

SAILING SMART

1

GETTING INVOLVED

THE STARTING LINE

When I was a small child, my father was working at a boat company in Williams Bay, Wisconsin, building sailboats and motor launches that would be used on Lake Geneva. We lived on Delavan Lake, just a few miles away. It was a quiet place then—no raucous outboards rushing around, no exuberant water-skiers.

One sunny June day, when I was five years old, my father brought home a small cedar-planked, canvas-covered dinghy. We went down to the dock, he gave me a few simple instructions, and then pushed me off. That was all there was to it. I sailed away from the dock in a more or less straight line, turned around, and sailed back. I got a few more lessons over the next couple of days, but I already had plenty of confidence in what I was doing. And of course I had no trouble getting friends to come with me, for we all discovered this boat was a great mode of transportation. We could visit the kids on the other side of the lake or around the point. And sailing was certainly a lot more fun than walking.

The boat's small sail wasn't in the best shape, so I decided to repair it by using one of my mother's sheets to patch the spot where the mice had lived the previous winter. Then I put a sign up on a tree and advertised sailboat rides for ten cents. In about two weeks I had saved enough money to get the old sail repaired professionally. And by the end of the summer, I had saved enough to buy a new cotton sail from Joy Brothers, a famous sailmaker in Milwaukee.

One year later I was allowed to race seriously. I started out as a crew on one of the big cedar-planked scows that used to race on all the inland lakes. They all leaked like sieves in August when their topsides dried out. But I wanted to get involved in racing, so I soon found myself down in the bilge with a pump and a bucket in my hand. After the start, going up to the windward mark, it wasn't long before I was down there pumping like mad and trying to keep the boat up on top of the water rather than at the bottom of the lake. And when we would pass someone, all the rest of the crew up on the weather rail would start cheering and hollering, and that just got me pumping and sponging all the harder.

Then, after the race was over and we were sailing home, someone asked me, "Hey Buddy, do you want to steer?" And that's how I got my first chance to steer one of those beautiful fast boats in a breeze under a full spread of sail. I will always remember what a thrill it was for me to hold the tiller of that racing boat in my hand.

That winter I began to get involved with iceboats, another new experience. In iceboating you have to orient yourself quickly to a wind which you cannot see blowing over the ice, but which you know is always there. My father put me into an iceboat and once again I was pushed off from the shore. Because of my summer sailing experience, I knew enough about which way the wind was blowing to orient myself and get my sail pulling correctly.

My father never really emphasized boat tune when he was teaching me to sail and to race. He basically worked on only three things: steering, sheet tension, and concentration. And it is funny, but in spite of all the sophisticated advances in sailboat equipment, those three things are still the most important elements to work on in sailing. My father also instilled in me a solid desire for competition and a commitment to diligent practice. He was a hard taskmaster: he was never impressed by second-place finishes. He impressed upon me the importance of caring for my equipment and having everything ready to go well before the start of a race.

When I was eleven I started to race my own boat on Delavan Lake. My father would come down and watch me from the edge of the lake. And that evening at dinner he would tell me what I had done well and what wasn't quite so good. He always knew what had happened during the race and what I had done incorrectly. And, after the dishes had been cleared, he would put the salt and pepper shakers on the table: the buoys. Spoons became the boats, and then the lesson would begin. Pretty soon the tears would be running down my face and my mother would tell my father not to be so hard. But he would bring his fist down on the table and say to her, "Buddy's got to learn. He can't be making the same mistakes over and over!"

A year later, three crews from Delavan, including myself, went over to Lake Mendota at Madison, Wisconsin, at the end of the summer to sail in the Inland Lake Yachting Association's X Class championship. There were about seventy boats there—my first really big regatta. When it was over, the three Delavan crews had finished first, second, and third. Even though all of us were relatively inexperienced, we did so well because we had spent all summer out on the water with our boats. We had put in the necessary practice time.

I was actually leading the regatta until I ran into the leeward mark during the last race. Though there was a funny sea condition at the mark, to this day I'm still not sure what happened. All of a sudden I saw that I had ticked the buoy. In those days the racing rules said that if you hit a buoy you were automatically disqualified, so I just turned the boat around and headed for the shore. I had a two-hundred-yard lead and nobody even saw the infraction. In fact, when I headed for home the judges came over and made a big fuss about it. But my father had driven it into me that the only way you sail a race is the honest way. And the passage of time hasn't changed that one bit.

By the time I was sixteen, my family had moved to Lake Geneva, where I still live. I was sailing fairly well, I thought, but then I went to one regatta where I made the same mistake on the starting line three times in a row. My father was there, and he started to give me what he thought was some helpful advice on how to correct the problem. I was too old and too smart to accept his advice without some argu-ment. I had only managed to get about three sentences out of my mouth when he said, "All right, kid. That's enough. To-morrow I get on the boat with you."

The next day we went out for the race and he began to work on my starting procedures. He told me in no uncertain terms to get up on the starting line, and he was being so forceful about what he was saying that I began to get pretty angry myself. Sure enough, off we went at the gun right in the first wave of boats—the first time I had been able to do that correctly during the entire regatta. We went off in great style, got to the windward mark in fifth place, and went around the course passing boat after boat until we won the race by a comfortable margin. Then my father turned to me, smiled, and said, "All right, kid, that's more like it." What I learned from that experience was that my father *knew* how to get a boat up on the starting line, while I only *thought* I knew.

THE MALLORYS

When I was twenty I could sail on a par with anyone on the inland lakes and could beat them more often than they could beat me. I had heard about the Mallory Cup, which is the Men's Sailing Championship of North America, and thought that it would be a great challenge to compete against sailors who came from different parts of the country. So I decided to get into the eliminations. I went down to Chicago to see Jack Shethar, who had grown up in the competitive sailing envi-ronment of Long Island Sound but was working in Chicago at the time. I asked him if he would sail with me, for I knew how impressive his tactical ability and sailing skills were.

He came on board and he immediately said that he didn't want to see anyone looking into the bottom of the boat. All of us, he said, were to keep our eyes and our thoughts up on the course ahead of us. There wasn't any need for someone to waste time looking into the bilge. Jack was a genius when it came to tactics, and we managed to win our regional eliminations for the Mallory with relative ease.

I learned a great deal about tactics from sailing in those Mallory competitions. It is a swap-boat series, with each crew rotating so they sailed one race in every boat. I participated in five consecutive Mallory Cup events and won the last three of them, which is something that hasn't been done since.

But the first two Mallorys I sailed in were a different story. The first was held in Seattle, where I found myself sailing against Ted Hood, Bus Mosbacher, Bill Ficker, and Gilbert Gray—all of them extraordinary sailors. I had all sorts of trouble in that first event, even though our crew was the best from the inland-lake area. But when I was ashore I kept my eyes and ears open and I listened very carefully to everything that was being said. And I learned a lot.

The following year the Mallorys were held in Marblehead, Massachusetts, and George O'Day was competing that year. He was without question one of the most formidable downwind sailors I had ever seen. And though he usually got to the windward mark last in the fleet, he and his crew knew how to sail off the wind so well that they sailed right by everyone and invariably finished in first place.

George O'Day taught me at that Mallory regatta that there is a whole lot more to racing than just sailing up to the windward mark and then, after you are around, reaching down for the ham sandwich and soft drink. George O'Day taught me about an entirely new set of challenges that come up when you are sailing off the wind. And when I got back to Lake Geneva after that second Mallory series, I thought about what George had said, and I took my boat out and started to sail. And I did nothing but sail downwind. I began to practice how to sail using the apparent wind. At the time I didn't fully understand what was happening, but all of a sudden I started to go faster off the wind. What I was learning to do was to keep the wind flowing across my sails whenever I was running free.

The result was that when we went to Texas the next year for our third Mallory, we just managed to win in a very close competition. But we had won in a keelboat, which was especially gratifying because it was the first time I had ever really sailed a boat of this type. At the awards ceremony we invited all the crews to come up to Lake Geneva the following year. We had eight brand-new E Scows for the series, and I managed to win the qualifier again. In that particular Mallory regatta we showed everyone how to sail downwind in the same style that George O'Day had used to burn me so badly a couple of years earlier. I think my winning score in that year's Mallory stands as the largest margin in the history of the event, just as our score in Texas the previous year was the smallest in the event's history.

The following year we went up to Montreal to sail what was to be my final Mallory series. It was sailed in Dragons and the weather was a mixed bag, with heavy air for some of the races and light air for others. Actually it was ideal for a round-robin series like the Mallory: the constantly shifting conditions force you to change your own gears quickly; you must know what your sail shapes should be for the variable wind and water conditions. We won that event too, which made it three in a row.

OLYMPIC COMPETITION

Not long after that last Mallory, Bill Bentsen, whom I had known and sailed with on Lake Geneva, suggested that we consider getting into an Olympic-class boat. Having grown up in a small community in the Midwest, I had never given much thought to entering the Olympic Games. Well, after thinking about it for a while, Bill and I got ourselves a Flying Dutchman, a high-performance, two-man dinghy that is still an

Olympic-class boat. We had only sailed the boat twice before we headed off for Chicago and a big regatta in which all the best sailors in the class were competing.

When we got there, everybody was setting up their rigs, looking at their sails, and fiddling with this string and tweaking that one. When I saw all those goings-on I turned to Bill and whispered, "Boy, are we out of touch!" But he answered right back, "Don't be too sure about that." And he was right. In the first race we were right up with the best of them beating up to the windward mark. And we lost out on the reaches only because we weren't used to sailing a high-performance boat that didn't weigh much more than a popcorn ball.

So we went back to Lake Geneva and once again began to work on our offwind sailing. In fact, we worked on it all winter out on the lake. It was the first time in my memory that the lake hadn't frozen over completely. Out we would go, in that ice-cold water, with our rubber suits and boots. We practiced sailing off the wind, then turned around, beat back up, and went downwind again. Things froze up on the boat and I began to think the whole project was getting pretty ridiculous. But Bill said we had to do it, and that was that. Bill showed me that winter how important it is to plan, and then carry out, a thorough program of training and practice.

We spent all winter out on Lake Geneva in our rubber suits. But the amazing thing is that after a while, our practice sessions got to be interesting. Then they got to be fun, and not long after that we started to make real progress. Through those hard winter practice sessions we learned how to beat, how to reach, and how to go downwind in a Flying Dutchman.

When the Olympic Trials came around six months later, we did so well that we didn't even have to compete in the last race of the Trials. Our hard work that winter had paid off for us. We had made the United States Olympic team, and now Bill and I were off for Japan and the Olympic Games.

But we gave ourselves a major handicap before we even got on the water. Assuming (incorrectly) that certain modifications were required, we went to Japan with a boat that was

forty pounds overweight. One thing I learned from that experience is that if you are competing in a class boat, you must
always study all the specifications and potential design problems well in advance to avoid getting caught in a situation
where you are not sure what a rule change will do to the
performance of your boat.

I learned a couple of other tough lessons in Japan during
the actual Olympic races. We capsized in one race when the
wind was blowing around 35 knots. We had the spinnaker up
and didn't bother to take it down before we righted the boat.
Of course, once the boat was righted, the flapping and water-
logged sail blew the boat right over again. We finally did
secure the spinnaker, righted the boat again, and continued
racing. Then the rudder broke. In spite of all this we still were
in fifth place. But when the rudder snapped we gybed, capsized, and the mast jumped its step and went through the
bottom of the boat. This time we were out of the race for
keeps.

I stayed up all night working on the boat while Bill worked
on the mast. We got only three hours of sleep before we had
to go out to race. We lost that one right on the finish line to
Hans Fogh, sailing for Denmark, and that loss was enough to
put the Gold Medal out of our reach. We had to settle for the
Bronze.

That heavy-weather race taught me that you must always
be able to think positively and clearly when a crisis occurs on
the water. In our case, when we first tipped over we should
have immediately realized that the speed of the wind was
making the race a battle for survival rather than a boat-
against-boat competition. And a third-place finish, or *any*
finish at all, in such a race would have been better than the
did-not-finish we had to score. We got that DNF not because
we sailed poorly, but because we were hasty and didn't think
the situation through.

I remembered that lesson a couple of years later in a Pan
American Games, when Bill and I got caught in a squall. We
ran into the back of a wave with such speed that we capsized,
and the force was so great that the mast bent. This time we

played it safe: we took the jib down and sailed around the course with just the mainsail up. When the race was over we found we were the only Flying Dutchman that had completed the race. We scored the big points instead of receiving a did-not-finish.

Not long after those Pan American Games, Bill and I went up to the Flying Dutchman World Championships in Montreal. During that regatta I saw techniques of rocking and sculling in light air that I simply could not believe. If you angle up the rudder of a Flying Dutchman, or any boat for that matter, the propulsion you can get from sculling is incredible. Unfortunately all these techniques can be very helpful in light air, though they are not allowed under the rules.

Because I knew that the next Olympic Games in Acapulco, Mexico, were going to be sailed in light air, I decided it was time for me to get out of the Flying Dutchman class. I didn't see how the international situation with regard to the light-air antics I had seen in Montreal was going to get better. I had put a lot of effort into honest sailing over the years, but it seemed some of my competitors in the class at that time didn't agree with me. So I withdrew entirely from sailing for about two and a half years. Even though I did have some very happy moments in the Flying Dutchman, I do have to say that I left that class on a sour note. And even today I feel badly about leaving the Flying Dutchman without having had an opportunity to put something back into the class for all the good times it gave me.

But when the International Yacht Racing Union voted to give Olympic status to the Soling, a three-man keelboat, Bill Bentsen and I decided to team up once again for another Olympic effort. Not surprisingly, the techniques we had developed when we launched our previous Olympic campaign helped us to get back into the swing of serious practice sessions after being away from it for several years.

I got a Soling hull from a French builder and I decided to design my own rigging and deck layout. When I was finished putting the hardware on the boat, there was no doubt in my mind that what I had done was very different from what all the other Solings were doing. Bill and I drove the boat up to Kingston, Ontario, for an Olympic-class regatta, and we created quite a stir when we arrived in the parking lot. For one thing, we had no winches on the boat. Instead, there were Harken ball-bearing blocks and ratchets that handled all the wire rigging. And the sail-trimming lines were all placed under the decks. In all honesty I thought the boat looked like a thoroughbred sitting among a bunch of draft horses.

Our third crew, Bill Allen, flew in from Minneapolis and off we went, the three of us sailing together for the first time. It had been a long, long time since I had been racing in a keelboat and the result was that I badly misjudged my starts. Naturally this put us right back in the third wave of boats at the starting gun. But even with my bad starts we just sailed through everyone and won every race by a big margin. It was certainly an exciting return to the world of international competition.

We continued to work on our deck layout and to modify its mechanics right up to the Olympic Trials, which, for the Soling, were being held in San Francisco. This time there wasn't anything we hadn't looked into and we were ready for everything that might happen. The gear was polished and tuned on the boat, we had gathered all the information about local wind and water conditions at the Trial site, and we knew how to analyze our current readings. We even went to the Army Corps of Engineers, which maintains a scale model of San Francisco Bay in its offices in Sausalito. We sat and watched the tide come in and out, and we made very careful notes. In short, we thought we had every aspect of the Trials set and under control. We thought we were prepared!

But right on the starting line of the first race I got into a battle with Bob Mosbacher at the leeward end of the line and I completely forgot everything I had learned in my prerace homework. The tide took me over the line early and I had to gybe around and come back on the port tack. At that point the rest of the fleet was sailing across in front of us. All of them were on the starboard tack and all were headed over to what was obviously the favored side of the course.

Despite a terrible start we still had enough boatspeed to be in third place as we approached the windward mark. But then I got into a tight maneuvering situation with another competitor and once again I forgot everything I had studied so hard to commit to memory. This time I forgot how strong the current could be. I hit the windward mark, had to re-round it, and when we settled down for the reach we were in eighteenth place! We finally managed to pull ourselves back up through the fleet to finish the race in fifth place.

In the second race, our mast broke. All the things we had planned for so carefully before the Trials were rapidly coming undone. We somehow managed to fix the mast, though, and settle down. Eventually, we did sail the way we knew we could, and when the Trials were over, we had won, and Bill Bentsen and I were on our way to Kiel, West Germany, for our second Olympics, with Bill Allen aboard as our hardworking third crewmember.

That year we were fortunate to have a tuneup boat accompany us, and the crew—Bruce Goldsmith, Rob Lansing, and Bob Barton—were just terrific. They made us work hard for every inch of ground we could get from them, and their efforts during the weeks just before those Olympics had a significant bearing on our ability to win the Olympic Gold Medal in those Games.

That was also the year that Paul Elvström was racing a Soling in Olympic competition. It was the first and only time I have ever sailed against him. I think it is fair to say that he had as unfortunate a set of races as anyone there. And he had the added burden of being on the losing side of a protest right at the outset of the regatta, which put him in a box that he was never able to jump out of during the entire course of those Olympic Games.

Since the Kiel Olympics I've continued to race the Soling internationally, and more recently I have gotten involved with a lot of other classes, including the Star. All this racing has reinforced my belief that there never is just one way to do something on a sailboat or on the racecourse. There could be as many as three ways, and possibly even more than that. I still enjoy looking for the best way to make my sails set better, the most efficient way to lay out the deck hardware on my boat, and finally, the best way to get through the water quickly.

Once you have mastered these basic concepts, it is easy to transfer that knowledge to another kind of boat even if it is larger or smaller. The principles are exactly the same.

TAKING THE PLUNGE

One of the very nice things about sailing is that anyone can get involved. A farmer who lives out in my part of the country—the Midwest—might head down to the Caribbean for a vacation because he has had a good corn crop. While he is there he sees the kids out sailing boardboats and sailboards and he decides he would like to get out there too. After all, when he is home, he knows which way the wind is blowing: when the wind blows out of the south he can smell the hoghouse and when it is blowing from the north he can smell the cow barn! That's not difficult and he can relate to that. So he gets on a boat, he sails out to the reef and back. Then he does it again. When he gets back home, he goes out and buys a boat and starts to sail some more. Then he talks to some friends, and the next thing you know they've set up a sailing club on the local lake. It's happened a lot over the years, and I hope it continues to happen.

Getting involved with sailing isn't hard at all as long as you have some enthusiasm and drive. Don't worry about your physical size, because it doesn't have much to do with being a good sailor. You can weigh 280 pounds and be a good sailor and you can weigh 100 pounds and be just as good a sailor. Competitive sailing *is* an athletic sport, but the great thing about it is that size and weight don't have any bearing on how good or bad you are going to be. You can choose the class of boat best suited to your particular physical characteristics.

If you have the willpower to put in the necessary hours and

develop some expertise, you can be first in your club, then first in your district, first in the country and—who knows—first in the world. As you get older, you can switch from the faster dinghies to slower-reacting boats. You can even move on to an offshore boat where you can have your crew put up the sails and take them down again whenever you want to make a sail change.

There is no ceiling and there is no cellar in sailboat racing. Anyone can play: young or old, big or small.

I can honestly say that sailboat racing holds as much fascination for me now as it did when I sailed my first boat. I was a pretty good little sailboat racer by the time I was eleven, and now, some forty years later, I'm still able to compete successfully at the world-class level. There aren't many sports around where you can be competitive over so long a span of time. Getting out and sailing, and racing, can be something you can enjoy all your life.

However, if you want to develop, hone, and maintain your racing skills, I believe that you should never stray too far from one-design and small-boat racing. A small boat forces you to pay attention to the wind and water and gives you a clear feel for its own motion. In a small boat you quickly learn about the effect tiller movement has on the boat and you get an immediate reaction to different sail shapes and crew positions. Best of all, when you sail on a one-design boat there is never any question in your own mind but that you win or lose because of your own sailing ability and your skill in reading the race course.

ONE-DESIGN SAILING

Though I have done some ocean racing, I prefer to compete in the one-design classes, where it is boat against boat, crew against crew, and all the rest of the detail is unimportant because everyone is using the same equipment. I have never been very thrilled by being matched up to some rating rule or formula, because in many cases you can be beaten even before you leave the dock. If the wind is blowing at a particular speed, the handwriting is already on the wall for some of the boats; it doesn't make a big difference how well or poorly that crew sails, because winning or losing will depend almost entirely on the special characteristics that have been designed into the boat. It seems to me that the only thing you can look forward to in that kind of race is the thrill and excitement of seeing what the next weather map is going to look like. On top of that, I am not sure I see the need to go to bed cold and wet, which is what often can happen when you sail offshore.

Sailing in a one-design race, on the other hand, is like being a sprinter in a hundred-yard dash. You're putting out a tremendous amount of energy for a short time. And when the race is over, you can savor your victory or defeat, recharge your batteries, and look forward to going out and sailing your next race. One-design racing has its own style and pace, which is essentially short and very intense. You give it everything you have for a relatively brief period, and there is never any question that you may have won or lost because of some computer program. It is your own skill and ability that is going to get you up to that finish line either ahead or astern of your competitors.

USE WHAT YOU HAVE

If you really want to get involved in successful sailing, the first thing you must do, even before you get out on your boat, is to start tuning up your senses of sight, smell, balance, hearing, and what I call your sixth sense: your ability to anticipate and make all the necessary adjustments to the wind and sea conditions as well as to the competition. Good eyesight is important, of course, but you have to be able to relate it to what you are seeing out on the course. I've been in very few races where I couldn't identify a particular boat and crew from a considerable distance. And the reason I can usually do so is that I always make an effort to memorize what the individual crews I'm concerned with are wearing, or what color their sail numbers are. Small things like this can become very important in a large fleet when everyone gets spread out over the course on a beat to windward.

And I am also constantly on the lookout for things that "don't belong," because looking for them keeps me alert. Once I was hunting partridge with some friends and we had a guide with us. I was locating my share of birds, but our guide was just phenomenal in his ability to spot them. When someone asked him how he did it, he replied that he always looked for something that was out of place, that didn't belong. I've always remembered that, and when I am racing I am always on the lookout for buoys, boats, and anything else that just might not be in the proper place. This attitude has always helped me spot small but significant details very quickly.

Smell plays a crucial role in sailing. The point is well illustrated by an experience I had racing in a Flying Dutchman World Championship. It was just after the start, and I had two boats ahead of me to windward. All three of us were headed off on the starboard tack. I decided to tack over to port and cross astern of the others to see whether I could get out to windward. As I crossed their sterns I said to my crew, Bill Bentsen, "I think I smell a new wind coming in from a frontal system." He nodded to me, we went on another hundred yards or so to make sure we were in it, and then tacked back onto starboard. In thirty seconds we had the new breeze, Bill was out on the trapeze, and we had everyone beat by a mile at the first mark. And it was all because I was able to smell that new breeze heading my way.

In short, to do well in sailing you have to want to put all your tentacles out. When I am in a drifting match the first thing I do is take off as many clothes as I can. Everyone yells, "What are you trying to do, Buddy—get a suntan?" I answer, "Sure!" But what I am really doing is exposing as much of my skin as I can so I can quickly feel any changes in wind velocity.

In competitive sailing, many of the things you can do to improve your chances for victory don't have anything to do with sailing at all. For example, your own personal appear-

ance can have a big effect on your competitors. How you
dress, how you walk around the launching area, and how you
handle your own boat as you get it ready can have a considerable impact on your race results. Remember that it is important to establish yourself as a winner *before* any contest starts.
It can be done, and once you have people watching what you
are saying and doing, you have broken their own concentration and possibly disrupted their own preparation.

When I am at a regatta, I can tell a lot about my competitors by just watching how they handle themselves while
launching their boats. If I see someone who is all thumbs and
gets excited if things don't go just right as the boat is going
into the water, I remember that. It might have a bearing on
how I tackle that crew later on out on the course.

Finishing first in a sailboat race is great, but if you are going
to spend any time in this sport you are going to have to learn
how to live with a finishing position well behind the first-
place boat. After all, even in a fleet of just forty boats, the
odds of coming in first are heavily stacked against you. Don't
take defeat lightly, but do try to benefit in some way from
every race you compete in. I certainly haven't won every
race I've ever entered—far from it—but I am continually
learning something new, because no matter what the final
position, the race can be a valuable learning experience for a
serious competitive sailor.

And if you do start winning, don't ever be afraid to share
what you know with your fellow sailors. Every now and then I
see a one-design class getting into trouble, with the number of
boats in competition falling off. Almost invariably, this is
because those who are doing most of the winning are not
sharing what they know with the rest of the sailors in the
class. They are hoarding their knowledge. And because the
competitive cooperation is not there, the social side of the
competition isn't there either. And the inevitable result is
that when those winners stand up on the pedestal to get the
trophy, they are not really winners. These sailors forget that
unless there is a fleet of boats out there sailing with them,
there can be no race to win.

Keep listening to other sailors and keep learning about the sport from those around you. Don't forget that if you can sincerely congratulate someone who has done a better job than you have out on the course, and genuinely mean it, that is a sure sign that you have enough confidence in your own abilities to handle your own racing success when it does come. And that will be soon enough, once you really decide to get yourself involved.

2

PREPARING YOURSELF

I'm convinced most people *talk* themselves out of first-place finishes. They convince themselves that they have poor boat-speed. Or they tack right out of a perfectly good spot on the course and then blame it on a windshift they *thought* would come in. There's always something external, beyond their control, that seems to prevent them from winning any trophies. But the real reason these people are continually disappointed is that they are not mentally prepared to win.

They *know* they haven't done all the things they must do before they can be psychologically ready to succeed—so they make up excuses. I find that whenever I am mentally prepared, I automatically become a much smarter sailor than I am when I am not sure about how thorough my preparation has been.

When it comes to trying out something new, I never rush into it. I like to do something, think about it for a while, and evaluate whether it is a legitimate step forward or a step back. When I first got deeply involved with the Star several years ago, what I should have done was take a full week to design an ideal rigging and deck layout for the boat. And then I should have gone out and seen how it went on the water. But I didn't do it that way; I let almost an entire summer go by, putting the whole project to one side. Then suddenly I noticed that the date for the Star World Championships in San Francisco was only about a month away. I had so little time to put the boat together that if it weren't for the fact that my crew, Andreas Josenhans, helped me install the boat's layout and control systems, our preparation would have been a total disaster. We both knew how every one of those lines worked, where it led, and how it was anchored, so if something broke or let go, either one of us could have immediately gone to the source of trouble and made the repair. But that was the *only* thing about my preparation for those Worlds that was right.

In San Francisco we went out sailing not for boatspeed but to use what little practice time we had left to see whether the system worked. And that is when my mistakes began to show up. We broke the boom, and we wrenched a spreader when a backstay caught on it. We still were changing little things on the boat at five o'clock the night before the first race. There we were, with our heads in the bilge looking at each other, and I was saying to myself that I should have done all this months ago. All this last-minute preparation was totally contrary to what I had always believed in.

But then, in spite of all the problems that we had dealt with since our arrival, something came over me. I didn't say a word then to Andreas, who was still down in the bilge making some final adjustments. But later, as we walked away from the boat, I turned around, looked back at the boat, and said to him, "Hey, this time I am ready."

The point is, you've got to be able to say to yourself, and be honest about it, that you are ready to win. As it turned out we did go on and take that world championship.

In spite of my lack of concentration that particular summer, I do believe that it is vitally important to prepare yourself thoroughly, as well as your boat. Those who like to play down the physical aspect of training are only fooling themselves, and they can laugh about it as much as they want from their position in the fifth or sixth wave of boats that come across the finish line. Good physical conditioning *does* make a difference, especially on the last beat to finish. The one thing I don't like to see is a skipper, or crew, who gets tired and can't perform. What happens then is obvious: the tired skipper inevitably stops thinking clearly, and the result is that boat doesn't go as fast. And the minute tiredness sets in, the chances are very good that chills will rapidly follow, and unless you are lucky enough to be sailing in tropical waters, this will make the problem even worse.

GETTING INTO SHAPE

The kind of physical training required depends to a great extent on your age and the type of boat you are sailing. Perhaps the best and most obvious way to proceed is to sail yourself into shape. When you do this you use exactly the muscles you need to maintain proper body control. And surely, body control, posture, and balance are very important skills to have—especially in small-boat sailing. You will see sailors on every racecourse in contortions that would break the back of a snake. Particularly if you are a skipper, it's very important that your backbone remain straight and perpendicular to the water. This position keeps your head level with the horizon as you look straight ahead, from side to side, or up at the sail. Your head must always be held perpendicular to the horizon so that you don't get any of your angles distorted.

Many people develop back problems simply because their stomach and back muscles are not properly toned up. They compensate by slumping over as they sail. That position can hurt their lower back even worse, as well as impair their ability to keep the horizon on a level plane. For small-boat sailing, exercises done ashore can be very helpful. Bent-knee situps can do wonders for your back and stomach muscles.

How extensive a conditioning program you undertake is up to you. But remember that on the first windward leg, everyone is more-or-less equal and competitive. It is the *last* windward leg, the one that leads to the finish, where the difference between winning and losing may depend on your physical conditioning. Keep that in mind and develop your training program accordingly.

You should do some running, arm exercises, and limbering-up exercises as well. Some more-sophisticated programs might include swimming, and stretching exercises, along with games like squash, handball, or basketball. Anything that helps you develop quick reflexes, good body flexibility, and solid hand-eye coordination is going to help. Stretching exercises are especially beneficial, and swimming is a good way to work on your muscle extension. Also, if you are a small-boat sailor, keep your neck muscles nice and limber by practicing turning your head from one side to the other as far as it will go. This is very important, because on a racecourse you have to see what is going on around you in the peripheral areas without jerking the rest of your body around.

TRAINING YOUR EYES

Even if you have perfect vision, you have to train yourself to use your eyes, and this takes practice. First, learn what it is you should be looking for. Is it a mark, a puff of wind coming at you, a header, or a lifting breeze? Everyone can see some of these things, but they can't always decide what they should do with the information. You can practice making these kinds of decisions by looking at a mark to windward and decoding what the best way is to get there, based on the wind patterns you see. The same thing applies to seeing a developing tactical situation on the racecourse. You have to learn how to visualize ways you can protect yourself with an offensive or a defensive maneuver.

If you are behind, you have to analyze how you can work your way through the boats ahead of you. If you go into the windward mark on a starboard tack and four boats tack right on top of you as you approach the mark, you haven't "seen" and then thought through your final approach correctly. You haven't set yourself up properly in terms of those other boats, and you haven't done so half a mile to leeward of the mark.

There is really only one way to train your eyes to pick these things up, and that is to spend time on the water. Then when you do see something, you will have the experience to interpret it, and you can quickly respond with a prerehearsed course of action.

Sunglasses are excellent for watching approaching wind on the water because they heighten the contrast made by the ripples. The water tends to darken as the wind increases, and this makes a puff much easier to see.

Get used to looking for all the things that are coming at you, no matter whether they are puffs of wind, waves, or other boats. When you are actively looking ahead you always see things much sooner than if you are just sitting there staring at your bow as it goes through the water.

CLOTHING

When I was in the army, I was always told that I should wear my clothes loose and in layers if I wanted to keep warm. And that doctrine also makes good sense for sailors. I have never been able to sail very well in a wet suit because it restricts my head movements. Instead, I like to wear a flannellike garment over a T-shirt. The flannel drains water quite well, and even if it does get wet it still keeps me warm. On top of these "woolies" I might wear a pair of heavy duck canvas pants and a sweater, and over that I like to wear a one-piece waterproof suit. If you are sailing in bigger boats and the water is warm enough, a two-piece set of foul-weather gear should be adequate.

The amount of clothing you wear is dictated by the water and air temperatures you are dealing with. But whatever you wear must provide some body warmth and windbreaking ability, along with moisture resistance. Windbreaking is the most important, because if you are wet and the wind is blowing through your clothing, the moisture will evaporate— and that can really get you cold quickly. And when you start getting cold you use all your strength shivering to get warm, and pretty soon you can't function at all.

If you are traveling to an area that is going to be colder than your home waters, prepare yourself ahead of time by getting the extra clothes you think you will need. Then soak the clothes in water and weigh them. You don't want to run the risk of being disqualified because your clothes weigh too much. And never be afraid to take all the extra clothing you think you *might* need out to the racecourse. If you haven't brought it with you, there's no way in the world that you are going to be able to put it on when the wind starts blowing and the temperature begins to drop.

Sailing a small high-performance boat, you are bound to be in situations that roughly parallel having someone spray a garden hose in your face all day. And that spray will have salt in it, which can sting your eyes. Eyeglasses can help. Many sailors now use a visor to shield the spray. I have always used a blue baseball cap with a short brim.

Seaboots are always proper gear. And if you are going to be sailing in cold weather, get a boot one size bigger than normal and wear them over a pair of heavy wool socks.

I don't like to wear gloves, for I lose the touch of the helm and the feel of the sheets—and these are the inputs that tell me when I am in the groove and when I am not. I recommend sailing with bare hands, because you get a better sense of what the boat is telling you. Working a piece of rope back and forth in your hands while you are ashore is one way to toughen them up. Squeezing a tennis ball builds up strength in the forearm, which will help for things like spinnaker work.

PRACTICE

How you practice aboard your boat is up to you, but certain basic maneuvers will have to be perfected before you get out onto the course. These basic moves are tacking, gybing, and going around marks. You must practice making a tack so many times that you and your crew can literally mark, on the floor of the boat, where the right foot goes, where the left foot goes, how you will hit the weather rail, and how everyone will get out over the side. This sequence must be executed the same way every time, or you are going to wind up losing ground to a crew that does the maneuver correctly.

I believe practicing by yourself is the best way to get these basic movements down. Keep in mind that the tacking maneuver, along with gybing and mark-rounding, can win more championships for you more consistently than any of the many fancy tactics some sailors like to use. Over the years I have practiced a great deal with just my own boat, and this system has helped me work on things like my tacking procedures and getting the boat back up to full speed quickly when the tack is completed. Because I do practice something like tacking more than most of my competitors, I know that when I start tacking against them they are going to be slower—even though they might have better speed through the water on a straight line.

Knowing you can do at least one thing better than your competitor is one of the most important edges you can have while racing. It's a nice feeling to know that you are able to make your competitor do something he doesn't want to do. In this case, one boat may be able to sail very fast on a tack that lasts a quarter of a mile. But if you start tacking every 100 yards, you can wear that boat down; it just can't tack as well or as quickly as you can. So another reason you should work hard on the basic maneuvers is to gain the confidence that you can do the basics better than anyone else. And when you can impress another crew with your tacks, gybes, and spinnaker sets, then you are going to have them looking at you instead of at their own boat. You will have them beaten, and they won't even know it!

If you are seriously interested in getting your maneuvers down, you have to know how your boat handles in every situation. One excellent way to learn your boat's turning characteristics is to practice an approach to a dock or a buoy. You start by sailing downwind past the dock or buoy one boat length away. As the stern passes the 90-degree angle the buoy makes with the wind, put the helm over hard and bring the boat around into the wind. If you have done everything

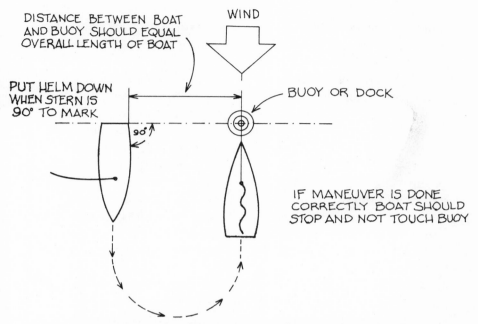

DISTANCE BETWEEN BOAT
AND BUOY SHOULD EQUAL
OVERALL LENGTH OF BOAT

WIND

PUT HELM DOWN
WHEN STERN IS
90° TO MARK

BUOY OR DOCK

90°

IF MANEUVER IS DONE
CORRECTLY BOAT SHOULD
STOP AND NOT TOUCH BUOY

Fig. 2-1. A good exercise to keep your boat's maneuvering characteristics fresh in your mind: Sail downwind past a dock or buoy, and then put the helm down hard and come around into the wind. You should be able to do this correctly no matter what the wind and sea conditions.

correctly, the boat will round up and stop in a head-to-wind position with the bow right at the dock or buoy. This is a drill that you should practice in all kinds of wind and sea conditions, and you should do it regularly to remind yourself how much headway you are going to have in any given condition (Fig. 2-1).

How early you begin your training for a local regatta or a world championship really depends on your background, how much knowledge you already have, and what type of boat you campaigned the previous year. If you are thinking of an Olympic effort, three years is not an excessive amount of time to sail in that Olympic class, and ten years of racing at all levels is the minimum amount of experience you should have logged in before making such an effort.

If you are trying for a regional championship and you have sailed in the same type of boat for a number of years, you might get by with only three weeks of after-work practices prior to the regatta—excluding several heavy weekend practices, of course. Ultimately every training period has to be an individual thing, and if you are competing in only one class you can pretty well keep track of what the competition is doing, and can act accordingly.

You might start out with a few local "telltale" regattas early in the season to see what you need to work on. Then you can go into a district regatta to see how you stand up against sailors you might not have seen before. That is a good time to check what new equipment is being used; that information will help you stay on top of new developments.

If it is possible, try to have someone come out for your training sessions with a powerboat. Whenever I am training for an international competition, I always try to have a powerboat come out with us. It is a great platform from which to look at sails, check the amount of twist and mast bend you *think* you have, and see how well the spinnaker is flying. Incidentally, when you are looking at a spinnaker, first look at it from close up, right alongside the boat. Then move out, perhaps a quarter of a mile away. Getting out this far lets you see exactly what the projection of the sail is and how the leech of the spinnaker is working with the underbody of the mainsail.

I am always a bit leery of photographs of sails, because a wave can change the set of a sail and one angle might create an entirely different perspective and give you a false reading. Viewing films, on the other hand, is an excellent way to see how a tack or spinnaker set might be done better.

Films, powerboats, etc., are very helpful, but they are luxuries. When your resources and time are limited, stay with your three basic boathandling drills: tacking, gybing, and mark-rounding.

It is not even necessary to have an actual mark to practice mark-rounding. All you need is to write down the direction of the true wind and then calculate what the various courses would be as you approach a mark and what course you would come to after you have gone around the mark. If you are working with an Olympic course, for example, you would head for the reach mark on a course that is 135 degrees off the true wind direction. Then, on a given signal, you would gybe the boat through 90 degrees, simulating the maneuvers you would perform at the reach mark, and keep going on the new gybe toward the mythical leeward mark. Then you might drop the spinnaker and come around hard onto the wind, just as you would at the actual leeward mark.

You can do this all day long if you want to. One thing all this course-changing will do is get you and your crew in the habit of looking at the compass right after a major course change. This helps you get on the new course faster, so you won't lose any distance on the new leg.

It is very helpful if you can arrange to have someone off in another boat when you're practicing mark-rounding. The observer can run a stopwatch and take notes on small but important details such as spinnaker-pole height and how the crew is using their hands. For example, you shouldn't have to put the spinnaker pole up, cleat it, then readjust it because you missed the proper height the first time. You should practice putting up the pole until you can cleat it, leave it, and get on to other things.

When scheduling practice sessions, the most important thing is to set a time *and stick to it.* Your crewmembers have other things to do in life, after all. Tell them that you are going sailing at five in the afternoon, you will return at six-thirty, and after that there will be a fifteen-minute recap session. Then stick to that schedule.

For the average crew in good condition, I think a training session that lasts an hour and a half to two hours is plenty, though if I had an hour-and-a-half session planned for the morning, I might also plan an afternoon practice that would last just as long. As soon as you are out in the practice area, go into your drills. You might do fifty tacks, fifty gybes, and twenty-five spinnaker sets to start off the session. Then practice finding the true wind. Then you might practice starting the boat from dead in the water and accelerating "through the gears" up to full speed. Follow that up with drills to stop the boat's motion through the water.

Make a practice starting line using some buoys, then work on your final approach up to the line. Have one member of the crew sight the two marks and call out when the bow is right on the line. When you are told the bow is on the line, immediately head off for the mark to leeward of you and have someone sight over the rudder post and backstay or the middle of the transom to see how far off the line you are. If you are exactly on the line, the buoy astern of you should be right in line with the rudder post or the middle of the stern.

If you are practicing for a major regatta and you are expecting sixty boats to be there, set your starting line so that it will be long enough to handle the sixty-boat fleet. You won't be seeing a short line in the race, so don't use one in your practice. As skipper, you must think of everything that might take place on the course: a slam gybe, a slam tack, a spinnaker set, and starting and stopping your boat. Practice all these maneuvers. You must know exactly how long it is going to take you to go from dead in the water to fifty yards away in any given wind strength. You should know it by instinct, as well as on a stopwatch.

You should also include roll tacking in your practice sessions. In this maneuver, you are trying to fool the wind by keeping the sails full longer as you go into the tack. You do this by hiking out and pulling the boat to windward on top of you as you start to tack. Then, as you come across on the new tack, the crew moves quickly to the new windward side and hikes out to bring the heel angle of the boat back up, in order to increase the apparent wind flow over the sails once more and also to lever the boat through the water to windward with the keel or centerboard.

Roll tacking requires exaggerated crew movements, which must be done smoothly or the motion of the rig in the wind and the motion of the keel or centerboard below the water will slow the boat down. Roll tacking is a perfect example of a maneuver that has got to be done the same way every time.

There never should be any need to talk about getting ready to tack, or gybe, after you have made the first twenty-five practice maneuvers in the spring. If my crew is out over the side in a practice session, I tack, and they wind up in the water, the only explanation is that they are not paying attention. During a race, if I think the attention on board my boat might be wandering, I will deliberately throw in one or two hard, fast tacks to get everyone back in the race. If I have to concentrate on steering the boat to windward, the crew shouldn't be thinking about the hot showers waiting for them ashore! Throw a surprise move or two into every practice session so that everyone stays alert, and most importantly, everyone knows how to turn a potential disaster into a perfectly controlled recovery.

Inevitably, there are going to be times in a practice session when everything you do seems to go poorly and everyone's timing is off. That is when you have to fall back on a basic principle people use when they are training a bird dog: Always finish every training session with a good retrieve. You can't let a puppy go home on a sour note even if it means just throwing a dummy bird out thirty feet in front of you on the bare ground, and then watching the dog stumble around until he finally finds it. At least he *has* found it, and now you all can go home happy. It's the same thing on board a racing boat. If things have been messed up all day but your time is up for this particular training session, set up a very simple drill. Then, when it is done right, stop and sail your crew home happy.

A skipper can make any crew look good at a mark-rounding, and he can also make them look bad. If you have been having trouble going around marks in a practice session, you should try one rounding where you do your best to help make the maneuver look good. Then wrap the session up and talk about how good that last rounding was on the sail home.

If you have a new crewmember on board, someone who

hasn't been practicing with you regularly, the best way to get that person through any practice is to talk him through all the basic maneuvers *before* you leave the dock. Point out the specific lines and control points and describe what is going to take place once the session begins. It is well worth taking the time to go through every maneuver in slow motion one or more times. If you start off describing things this way, they will come back much more easily in the actual practice, in which things move much more quickly. Take a little time *before* you go out because it is going to save you a lot of time later as you try to unravel the snarl you are sure to find yourself in when something isn't pulled up or eased off correctly.

If the wind is blowing hard, practice with your full racing gear and life jackets. It is something you will have to do during a race, so you might as well get to the point where the bulkier clothing becomes second nature to you. More and more I wear my life jacket no matter what the weather conditions; the latest jackets are fairly comfortable, and wearing one gives me additional peace of mind.

Two-Boat Training

Training with another boat is an excellent way to work on your sail-setting techniques and your boathandling. One good way to find out how well you are tacking is to have both boats start off on opposite tacks and sail close-hauled for one minute. Then each boat tacks and sails back toward the other. When the two boats meet, the lead boat may not tack on the wind of the boat astern and it must make a new tack at least once every minute. The boat astern, however, can tack at will. When both boats have made twenty-five or thirty tacks in a five-minute period in close quarters, there will be no question about which one is better at tacking. This is a good drill to use whenever you want to sharpen up your crewwork.

However, if you are sailing a parallel course with another boat and you are both working on sail shape and straight-line sailing for boatspeed, make sure you watch the compass so that you are not misled by a windshift that can change your course. That merely alters your relative positions.

When Bill Bentsen and I were just starting out in the Flying Dutchman, we were very good sailing to windward against our competition and we were equally good on the downwind legs. But we were dead slow on the close reaches. We knew that was our weak point, so we worked hard on that point of sail. We had a friend get out on the water with a movie camera and he took pictures of us. Then we talked a lot about what they showed. Up to that time we had a barrel of excuses about our slow speed: Bill was too light to be in the front of the boat; I was too heavy for the back; our weight was all wrong. What we learned from watching the movies was that our real problem was how we were setting up our sails and how I was steering the boat. Once we knew what our problems actually were, we set out to correct them. By working hard in each subsequent practice session to get the right sail and weight combinations, we got those close-reaching problems out of our system.

My point is that you are probably not going to be able to spot your own major weaknesses until you have someone watch you or take some movies, or until you get into a race and find out how well you are doing against your competition. After every training session (or race) make a point of sitting down with the crew ashore and talking things over for fifteen minutes or so and deciding where there can be improvement, either in procedures or in tactics. I do think it is up to the skipper to bring out the problem areas that need work. If there is to be any real improvement, the skipper must spend a good part of subsequent training sessions working on those problems.

If, for example, you know from your racing experience that you are losing ground to others on the reaching legs, you should work on those points of sail until you build your speed up so you know you can sail on a par with the leaders. In this kind of situation, a coach can really speed up the learning. A coach can watch from another boat and make notes. This person doesn't have to be a great sailor. All it takes is someone who is interested, has enough knowledge to spot the moderately rough edges, and can time the tacking, gybing, and spinnaker-setting.

I've already touched on some practice drills you can do to increase your boatspeed. But the really important thing is to be aware of your crew's strengths and weaknesses. If another crew is faster than you are in straight-line sailing, your best defense against that boat in a race is to start tacking (or gybing if you are sailing downwind) so your opponents have to do something they don't want to do. If you can make them do something they do not want to do, or do something you can do better, you have them beaten.

I don't happen to like making a whole lot of notes in a book after a practice session, but I know a lot of very successful sailors who do. Writing things down is a good way to make sure that when you do find a setting that works, you can come back to it without spending a lot of time looking for it again. Things I do write down in a notebook are all the corrections that must be made to the boat before the next training session: hardware items and things of that sort.

Getting Out of a Slump

If you ever think you are losing your touch, always go back and start right at the beginning. If I see I am not sailing as fast or as consistently as I have in the past, I go through every one of the potential problem areas. First I check the finish on the boat and make sure it is up to racing standard. Then I start sailing and I work on my steering, my sails, and my adjustments. If I think the problem is something that I am doing, I ask the crew what they think, and we work together to come up with a consensus. Once I have my answer, I will spend an entire training session, or more if necessary, getting the problem solved.

But the real point is that when things are not going as well as you think they could, don't go out looking for excuses. Go all the way back to the beginning and recheck *everything*. Step back, analyze, go through all the checkpoints, and then see whether your performance improves. If you do all this conscientiously, the chances are good that you will find out what the problem is.

If you are honest with yourself, you'll wind up saying things like "My boat won't track properly because I don't concentrate," "My boat doesn't foot because I don't sheet the sail properly," or "My boat doesn't point because I don't bend the mast properly." All these things are what I call *pilot error.* If people flew airplanes and drove cars the way they often sail their boats, they would be flying upside down and capsizing their automobiles.

One question that comes up regarding slumps is: Can a sailor or a crew peak too soon? The college basketball coach near my hometown has always won his share of big victories and he has always had successful seasons. But he says that he doesn't mind seeing his team lose to someone a week or two before the championship game. He says it's good for them, and I agree with him. The reason he thinks this way is that a loss often is the sign that a team has gotten overconfident. When you become overconfident in any sport, invariably you begin to let your guard down. An overconfident sailor gets too relaxed in his training drills; he stops studying his sails closely enough.

More than once I have said to my crew, "Hey, I think we are getting overconfident, and personally I don't think we are all that good because here is what we did wrong today." Then I recite at least ten things that could have been done better by everyone, including myself. What this does is bring everybody back down to reality. And, if things don't improve in the practice session the next day, I might deliberately do something like sail right up to the windward mark on port tack, come about at the very last minute, and then call for the spinnaker to be hoisted as I spin around the mark. Then I might decide to jump up and down, and I might even pound the deck for effect. A maneuver like this one can humble even the cockiest crew.

Use all your practice sessions to build up the level of concentration of every member of your crew. I sharpen my own concentration by thinking about all the leads on the boat, what effect they have on the sails, and what the sails look like after an adjustment. When I finish a practice session, or a race, I immediately resail the entire course in my mind. I think of all the good things we have done and I try to come up with solutions to any problems that have come up. As soon as we get home I always have a talk about the practice or race, and I immediately fix everything that is broken or needs to be modified. I never leave any repairs or changes for the following day, and my boat always is ready to sail again *before* I leave the launching area for home. Over the years I have learned that if you leave something undone it will worry you all the time it is broken and you can't enjoy the peace of mind and confidence that comes when you know the boat is ready to sail.

One thing you might do in practice to sharpen concentration is to have the crew exchange places with each other. I wouldn't do this too often, but it is a good idea to have each person on board handle the spinnaker through a gybe and learn how to get the spinnaker pole over to the other side. This gives everyone a feeling for all the problems that have to be overcome, what the other person's duties actually are, and most important, how they might be handled in a quicker or more efficient way. Everybody learns something in the exchange and you always come away with a little more understanding and sympathy for the responsibilities shared by the rest of the crew.

There's one habit I stick to in all my training sessions as well as on the day of the race. As skipper, I always sail the boat out to the course, and I always sail it back in. And I sail it as fast as I can. I don't want my racehorse to get any bad habits.

As a general rule, try to make your practice sessions a challenge to the entire crew. But never forget that the basics of tacking, gybing, spinnaker sets and takedowns, and mark-roundings have won far more races than tactics like heading out to one side of the course after a start, then quietly hoping for the windshift that will bring you into the windward mark in first place. It is the *basics* that win races. A boat with a finish that is smooth, gear and sails that work correctly, and maneuvers that all can be done instinctively by the crew is a boat that will be a consistent winner.

Mix up the sequence of your on-the-water drills to maintain a certain amount of freshness in the routine. It keeps everyone on his toes. But no matter what happens, don't forget to end every practice session the same way a good dog trainer does—on a good retrieve! Then sail for home on a high note. This produces the kind of music that I have found always carries over to the next time you get together again and go sailing.

SAILING TO WINDWARD

If you are ever going to be a successful sailor, you must be able to sail your boat to windward well enough to be competitive with the other boats. Sailing on a close-hauled course is probably one of the toughest things to do well, and that is why there is often such a great separation between boats on the upwind legs. Furthermore, most racecourses are weighted so you have to sail a greater distance to windward than you do on any other leg. So it's crucial to spend time mastering the techniques involved in sailing on the wind.

The first thing you must determine is your boat's optimum angle of heel. This angle varies quite widely from class to class or from one design to another, but it always applies, no matter how strong or weak the wind, and you should memorize what the angle is. A Flying Dutchman, like most dinghy-type boats, likes to sail to windward almost straight up with no heel at all. Keelboats, on the other hand, might sail at their best when they are heeled over as much as 20 degrees or more.

Whenever I get on board a boat I haven't sailed before, I sail off by myself and find out what the correct angle is. The boat will give you the information you need: straighten the boat up and it slows down; heel it over too far and it slows down—in short, whenever it gets off its ideal sailing lines it

slows down. Once you have identified the optimum angle of
heel, that becomes the *groove angle* of the boat; you always
should sail to windward at that angle. All your tiller, traveler,
and sail-shape adjustments should be made to keep the boat
sailing at that one angle.

An easy way to use this groove angle is to establish what I
call a *preferred horizon.* This horizon is the one I get when I
look forward over the deck and the bow to the horizontal line
made by the land or the water. Then I look at the intersecting
angle the deck and headstay (or mast) make with the horizon,
and that is the angle I memorize (Fig. 2-2). Once I have that
angle I go to it quickly after every tack. Or, when I am sailing
along on the wind and I feel the boat wanting either to heel
over or to straighten up, I can make the necessary corrections
to keep the boat sailing at precisely that angle.

Always steer with a relaxed hand when sailing on the wind. A
tight grip on the tiller or wheel only chokes the boat and
prevents it from telling you what the correct angle of heel is
and how it wants to swim through the waves.

And speaking of waves, you always want to help the boat,
with tiller movements if necessary, to go up the face of a wave
and down the back of a wave. In a short, choppy sea you often
can help the boat go through the waves by accentuating what
the helm is already doing naturally as the water flows by the
rudder. Many times I have picked up a lot of speed by
accentuating these helm movements. (Don't confuse this with
tiller sawing—a back-and-forth motion—which only serves to
slow the boat down.)

I like to maintain just a bit of weather helm, because that
helps the boat work up closer to the wind. If your helm is
neutral you have what I call a *dead fish* helm, which means
that the boat has lost its ability to properly track through the
water. The amount of heel a boat has affects the amount of
helm you get, and with most boats the greater the angle of
heel, the greater the weather helm.

But once you have set the sails up with the proper shape for
the conditions, you should use the main (and jib) traveler to

control your steering to windward. You use the traveler to keep your boat on its feet and sailing at the proper angle. In any oscillating wind conditions, where the wind is rising and falling, the first control you should go to is the traveler; you should ease it out if the wind comes up and pull it in if the wind drops.

Fig. 2-2. Every boat has an ideal angle of heel when it is sailing to windward. Once you determine the angle, memorize the angle the mast or headstay makes with the horizon, and try to keep that angle constant when you are sailing on the wind.

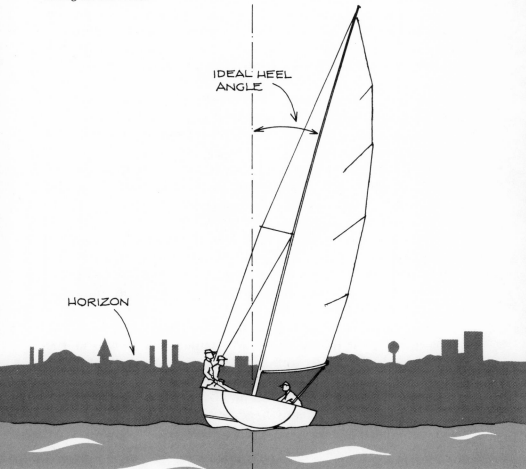

On many boats one crewmember is assigned to work the traveler, and it is in almost constant motion. When a big puff comes the traveler is eased down to leeward to maintain constant heel angle (in a very big puff the mainsheet can also be eased). Then, as the wind drops down again, the mainsheet can be brought back in first, then the traveler can be brought back up toward the centerline of the boat. (Incidentally, a traveler that is kept on the centerline always makes a boat sail poorly to windward in heavy seas. It will sail much more responsively if the traveler is at least several inches to leeward of the centerline.) If you can drop your traveler down on occasion to "open the gate," your steering range will be greatly increased. If you are going over waves, try dropping the traveler down as you head off the back of a wave. This can help keep the boat from heeling over as you turn away from the wind.

Good small-boat sailors work both the traveler and the mainsheet when sailing to windward, and occasionally they will release the mainsheet quickly then bring it back in again. Releasing the sheet trips the flow over the main for a second, but then the newly developed lifting power from the batten section can be used to help work up to windward, especially when the skipper is using a scalloping technique.

Scalloping is a devastating maneuver in most conditions except very light air. If you are sailing to windward in a moderate breeze with a flat sea, you should scallop to see whether you are sailing at your optimum in terms of speed, sail trim, crew position, and so forth.

The procedure for scalloping is as follows: Slowly head the boat down a bit below your close-hauled course and at the same time build some camber into the sails by easing both the jib and mainsheets a little bit. You will start to heel as you build up speed, but that speed now lets you come back up to course, go beyond it, and head even higher to windward, above your basic close-hauled course. Naturally as you go above the close-hauled course, you have to pull in your sheets (and travelers) again to get them working at the new and

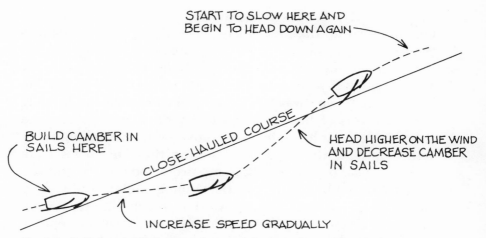

Fig. 2-3. Sailing a scalloping course to windward is an excellent technique to use in all conditions except very light airs to make sure you are sailing the best course to windward.

higher angle. Once you are above your course you can hang up there for a second or two before you begin to feel the boat stall and slow down again. Once you start slowing down, gradually head off again and ease the traveler down to get your sail camber back again for the next power drive (Fig. 2-3).

Scalloping like this is a good way to determine whether you are sailing on the best course to windward. It is essentially a very elongated snakelike course that can go as much as five to ten yards on either side of what you might consider your close-hauled course.

Scalloping is also a very effective tactic to use against an opponent, for it can throw off his timing. One minute he looks at you and you are heading off and footing through the water, and the next minute he looks you are pointing way above his close-hauled course. When he tries to adjust his course to your perceived course, without understanding what you are up to, he will find he has turned his boat radically in the water as he tries to sail the course you are steering. But he doesn't have the same speed or sail timing that you have. And if he tries to match your headings he will usually lose ground against you.

You must play the waves constantly. Look ahead, see them coming, turn up the face of the wave, then head off again as the back of the wave moves under the boat. You have to get involved with every wave and every change in wind velocity and direction if you are going to sail upwind correctly. When I am sailing to windward, I try and feel what the boat is telling me—in terms of how it wants to handle those waves—and then let the boat have the helm movements it is telling me it wants. And all the time I am getting these messages I am looking ahead over the deck to my preferred horizon to keep the heel of the boat at that critical sailing angle.

Sailing a keelboat to windward is much different from sailing a dinghy or a fast catamaran on the wind. With a keelboat you have to grind out the yardage a foot or two at a time. In a centerboard boat like a Flying Dutchman, 470, or Laser, you are sailing a quick-start-quick-stop machine. You can pick up two full boat lengths if you catch a wave properly. But you can lose four lengths if you don't.

But no matter what type boat you sail, you have to concentrate. You must be able to distinguish one wave from the next. Think what you are going to do with each of these waves and how you are going to steer past them—one by one. A wave can be an enemy to your boat and slow it down. But that same wave can also be made into a friend by using the proper steering technique as it comes by.

When I am sailing near other boats and I make the mistake of looking at them instead of the waves, my boat begins to buck like a bronco that wants to throw me off. A few seconds is all the time it takes to get out of phase with what is coming at me. Then I have to put myself back into the picture, get my sails reset, and begin to help my boat move again.

If you do lose your concentration, generally the best way to get your speed back is to drop the travelers down to leeward to power up the boat and regain your speed. Once you are back up to speed you can pull the travelers back up to where they were before you went to sleep.

Keep the crew as close together as possible and position the weight as close to the center of lateral resistance as you can. This reduces the tendency of the boat to pitch in the waves and helps it swim through them. Keeping this pitching to a minimum is a must in choppy conditions as well as when you are sailing in a dying breeze with a lot of swell left over.

This is also a good time to think about putting some twist in the upper sections of the mainsail and then heading off 5 to 10 degrees below a truly close-hauled course. You don't point quite as high, but you move through the water faster and as a result you make less leeway.

Look straight ahead. Watch for new wind patterns and keep that angle of heel constant. If the boat starts to heel, head up just a bit to keep the heel angle unchanged. And if you can see a band of wind approaching, you can anticipate when it will reach you and you can ease the boat up into the wind just a second or so earlier than you would have if you didn't know what was about to happen.

But don't neglect your peripheral vision. If you see a boat come into view out of the corner of your eye, immediately check your compass heading. If you are on a starboard tack and the boat appears on your weather quarter, are you being lifted? If you are not, you had better check your boat's tune, for the other boat is sailing faster than you are.

Telltales, Ticklers, and Flies

I happen to like telltales made from strands of yarn or light thread. I attach the lowest one about a foot from the heads of the crew when seated, and two more above that one, spaced about a foot apart. The idea is to be able to look straight ahead and see the telltale out of the corner of one eye and the luff of the mainsail in the other.

I've also seen ticklers on the luff of the jib on a lot of boats. The general rule is that if the inside one starts to flutter and stall, either you are heading too high or the jib is trimmed in too tight. Actually, I think too much emphasis is placed on jib ticklers and not enough on the shroud telltales. Since the shroud telltales do not rely on proper jib trim to be accurate, they give you the *real* direction of the wind as it comes at you.

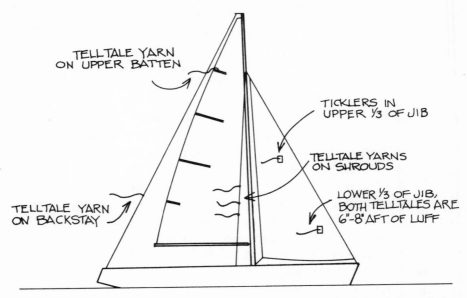

TELLTALE YARN
ON UPPER BATTEN

TICKLERS IN
UPPER ⅓ OF JIB

TELLTALE YARNS
ON SHROUDS

TELLTALE YARN
ON BACKSTAY

LOWER ⅓ OF JIB,
BOTH TELLTALES ARE
6"-8" AFT OF LUFF

Fig. 2-4. Telltales and jib ticklers are good indicators for determining wind direction. Both should be located so they can be easily seen from the helmsman's position. When in doubt, however, refer to the shroud telltales, for they do not rely on the trim of the jib for their accuracy.

I should add that I have never had a masthead fly on any one-design boat of mine. My reason is that if I want to look at the fly, I have to turn my head straight up. And if I have to do that I am afraid I will lose track of something that is happening, or is about to happen, on the boat. I might miss a wave, or I might miss a move a competitor is making astern of me.

However, I always like to look at the masthead flys on *other* boats. They can be a big help, particularly if I happen to be passing someone close aboard. All I have to do is to sight along the other boat's masthead fly to see whether I have passed through the wind shadow. If I am to leeward and the other boat's fly is pointing at me, I know I am still in disturbed air. If it is pointing behind me, I have already sailed through the other boat's wind shadow.

Telltales on a mainsail can be helpful, though it depends on the type of boat you sail. A piece of yarn tied to the top batten helps you find proper deflection. Also, mainsail telltales can help you determine how much boom vang you should carry off the wind. The yarn should flow smoothly in both upwind and offwind sailing (Fig. 2-4).

Years ago almost everyone steered sitting on the leeward side, but nowadays most sailors agree that there are too many factors that can hurt you if you sit down there. You can't see the wind or waves coming at you, and that means you miss all the subtle shifts, especially the lifts. You won't miss the headers because the jib ticklers are going to tell you that. But if you are sitting to leeward and watching your jib you have to be constantly testing the amount of possible lift by using your helm.

When you sit to windward you can see the shroud telltales, you can see the jib ticklers, and I think you are much more aware of what is coming down the road at you. But if you get in a tunnel of love with your jib ticklers, you'll inevitably lose the wave action and, eventually, the big picture. If I am sailing in very light air I might sit down in the cockpit or in the middle of the boat so I can see the mainsail and jib shapes easily and also keep track of the boats both to leeward and to windward of me. Sitting down also helps reduce wind resistance.

Trapezing

Poor trapeze work, otherwise known as the outhouse crouch, has lost more races for more sailors than you might think. You are guilty of it any time you are out on your trapeze with your fanny extending farther outboard than your back. Anyone who takes this position might be having a great time out on the wire but the leverage being produced is nothing to cheer about (Fig. 2-5).

The best trapeze position is parallel to the water from the waist to the head. If you are out on the trapeze and you feel you need to come back toward the boat to reduce the leverage, just bend your knees and move closer to the boat; don't straighten up at the waist.

If you are the helmsman on a trapeze boat, try to sail so that

Fig. 2-5. Getting out on the wire might feel exhilarating, but if you are in the outhouse crouch you are producing only a small portion of the leverage that is required. You get the full leverage only when you extend yourself out in the horizontal position.

the rear end of your crew goes just over the tops of the waves. The correct helm motion is one that establishes an in-and-out-of-the-wave pattern. Always look ahead at the wind on the water, for the real art of sailing a trapeze boat involves coordinating your steering with the wind.

Don't assume that the trapeze is a magic tool and that therefore the crew should remain out in the harness at all times. If you sail 60 to 70 degrees to the wind just to keep the crew out on the wire, instead of sailing the more standard 45 degrees, you'll soon find yourself sailing at 90 degrees to the mark and you won't be going anywhere—at least as far as the windward mark is concerned.

When you are out in the harness, keep your weight right over the centerboard. Look at the boat when it's out of the water with the board down and it will be easy to see where your feet ought to be spotted on the rail. Usually your front leg will be right next to the side shrouds when you are sailing on the wind. When you come into the boat do not come straight in. Instead, try swinging aft a little bit toward the skipper, bend your knees slightly, and put your aft hand on the rail for support.

Tacking

When and how you tack are very important elements in upwind sailing. Even if you make a good tack, in a sloppy sea you can lose at least one boat length every time you come around. The point is that you should tack only when the wind requires it: when you are in a known oscillating pattern and have to go with the flow, or you are forced to tack because you have another boat on top of you giving you bad air.

Most boats tack in about 90 degrees, so I think it's a good idea to break your tack into three sections with 30 degrees in each section. For the first 30 degrees, keep only a slow and gentle motion on the helm. Just squeeze up the first 15 degrees as the boat comes slowly up onto the wind. For the second 30 degrees make your helm angle far sharper as you come through the eye of the wind. Enter the last 30 degrees with decreased helm angle, and make the last 15 degrees just a squeeze down onto the new course (Fig. 2-6).

Fig. 2-6. Making an ideal tack involves breaking the tack into sections, then applying varying amounts of helm angle to the various components. The higher the wind, the more the helm can be squeezed at the beginning. With less wind, use a smaller amount of squeeze.

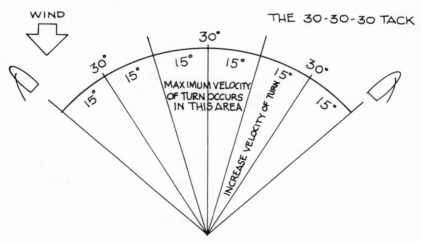

If you are in a small boat, when the first 30 degrees are completed the crew should heave themselves out to windward to begin the first part of the roll-tacking maneuver. As the boat passes the head-to-wind position, the crew should stay on the rail to heel the boat well beyond what is going to be the new heel angle on the new tack. But the moment the heel reaches the maximum angle the boat can safely assume, the crew should leave that side of the boat (now rapidly becoming the leeward side) and go up to the new windward rail in a fluid motion that keeps the angle of heel constant. If everything is done correctly and the sea is calm, hardly any speed is lost.

Never let your boat's bow fall off before you start your tack. I know some people feel this speeds the boat up and gets it around faster. But any time you sail away from the mark, the boat travels a greater distance—and some of it is to leeward. I think slowing the boat down by squeezing it up slowly at first is a far better trade-off than laying the boat off to increase speed, then doing a 90-degree turn all at once.

Another common mistake is easing the mainsheet as you start your tack, or even as you go through the second 30 degrees. This easing does nothing but slow the boat down and throw it off its proper heel angle. Don't ease your mainsheet until you get around to the final 30 degrees of your tack, or until the sails have come across the boat and have established their foil shape on the new tack. At that time you can ease both the main and the jib. When you do this you increase your camber and can quickly build up your boat speed to the speed you had on the previous tack. As your speed increases on the new tack you can trim the sails back in until they are back to the correct high-speed shape for the conditions you are sailing in.

On boats without self-tacking jibs, the jib sheet should never be released until the sail *wants* to go over to the other side because of wind on the sail. At that moment, and not until then, release the old sheet and quickly trim in the new one. Before the tack begins, don't forget to trim the new sheet in so that all excess slack has been taken out.

Once you are on the new tack, look at the angle that the mast, deck, and headstay make with the horizon, and make sure that it is at the optimum angle for upwind sailing. If the windward deck starts to rise up, come up into the wind just a bit to get that angle back down. Conversely, if the deck angle starts to drop as the mast straightens up, head off a little bit to get the angle back up. And keep checking and rechecking the wind direction by looking at the shroud telltales.

THE RACING RULES

When I was just beginning to race, my father always told me to remember that when the wind hit me from the right side I could keep sailing straight ahead, but when it came from my left side I had better watch out for the other boats. Well, that was fine, but I had to wait until I was eleven before I found out about something called buoy room. I was in a race and a kid hailed me for buoy room. I didn't think he was entitled to it but he convinced the judges later that he was, and my disqualification cost me first place in that regatta.

That experience has remained with me through all the racing I have done since, and my basic racing rule now is that I will never try to steer myself into a situation that I know might create a discussion after the race. I have two good reasons for this: The first is that any jam-up can easily affect my race results for the day, no matter who is right, because some other boat might sail around me as I am trying to get myself unsnarled. The second reason is that any protest immediately cuts down on my social hour after the race is over. And I don't really like to stand around and wait for my case to come up when I could be socializing and having fun with the rest of the sailors.

There is no question, though, that you ought to know the racing rules, and particularly the right-of-way rules. These latter are a precise set of instructions that, on the most basic level, are written to protect one boat from breaking the equipment of another. And it is true that the racing rules can also be used to win, or lose, a race or even a championship.

You can use the rules to shut the door on someone in a port-and-starboard situation at the finish line, for example. Or you can use the same port-and-starboard rules to send a competitor off to the wrong side of the course. And establishing an overlap at the two-boat-length circle as you approach a mark can save you many minutes of sailing as you attempt to pass the competitor ahead of you on a reach. If you can get that overlap, it is going to take you only one second to get past that boat.

You should also be aware of the fact that there are some sailors who like to spend time in the jury room trying to pick up places. They will stick their bow into a situation whenever they know they are right. Unfortunately they often fail to see that they are probably worse off, in terms of their overall fleet position, when they come out on the other side of the fracas.

In short, there are always going to be sensible and less-than-sensible sailors, and an important part of developing your own competitive strength is to know your opponents' strengths and weaknesses in this area. Some skippers, for example, are well acquainted with the rules and have considerable skill in handling juries and winning protests—even though they may never have won a championship. If you find yourself up against someone like this, I think it's a good idea to give this person a very wide berth. You stand to lose in any subsequent protest; but even more important, the fact is that whenever one boat is pressing a rule on another boat, both of them wind up losing ground to the boats around them. And that is why I use the racing rules only to avoid a collision or, if I am in World competition, to protect my position on the race course. In fact, I can't think of any time that I have ever given up my right-of-way position knowing that doing so would cost me either the race or even one position in that race.

It was only a couple of years ago, at a Star World Championship in Sweden, that I filed the first protest that I can remember. Another boat was trying to pass me to windward on a very close reach. I saw the other boat was very close and it was almost taunting us to do something. But that wasn't all it was doing: this boat was trying to take my position on the racecourse. So I gave the boat a fast luff, which I was perfectly entitled to do, we collided very gently, and of course I had right of way and the other boat was out of the race. I didn't have any malice in my heart when I protected my position and I don't want to brag about the fact that this was my first protest in many, many years. No, this is just one example of using the rules in a positive way to protect your legitimate position on the course against another boat.

But you can also use the racing rules creatively to improve your position—as long as you don't try to force yourself into a situation that is sure to cause a jam, and a discussion for the jury ashore later on. Once I was in a Soling championship and I was headed toward the leeward mark outside four other boats, all sailing abreast of each other. Each boat had an overlap on the other, and the skipper of the inside boat was yelling to all the rest of us that he had an overlap and therefore was entitled to room at the mark. I suddenly dropped my spinnaker, stopped my boat, and sailed across just astern of the four other boats. The inside boat was so preoccupied with telling all the other boats about its rights that I knew it was about to make a very poor mark-rounding. So I sailed right in between that boat and the mark. Sure enough, the skipper started telling me that I had no rights and I replied, "I know," and kept on sailing into what had now become a very large hole on the leeward side of mark. When I finally cleared the mark I had picked up those four places. And I had done so simply because I knew my own boat's characteristics, and I could see that my opponents were far more interested in telling everyone about their rights than in sailing their boats correctly. The rules, after all, don't have anything to do with developing boatspeed through the water. You are the one who can work on that.

3

PREPARING YOUR EQUIPMENT

FIND THE RIGHT BOAT

First think about a boat that fits your age group and your physical characteristics, and then think hard about your personality. What is it that makes a boat attractive to you? Are you happier with a simple or complex rig? Do you like to sail by yourself or with two or three others?

Keep in mind that some highly sophisticated boats can appear to be very simple to operate if all the mechanical advantages and leads are located under the deck and all you see on top are control lines. The boat may *look* simple to set up and sail, but it won't be.

I happen to enjoy sailing a scow—a relatively flat-bottomed boat that is very popular on the inland lakes. Part of the reason is that I grew up with the scow, but it also happens to be a boat that helps me sharpen my ability to determine optimum angle of heel. In a scow you quickly learn when you are in trouble and when you are all right. Because the bottom is relatively flat, there is a tremendous amount of the boat's surface that can be in the water. If you sail the scow with no heel at all you wind up going nowhere; heel a scow up and it comes to life.

A scow's helm is far less sensitive to heel angle than more conventional hulls, and this is what keeps my senses in tune. If the wind heels a keelboat way over and you don't make an adjustment, you have to pull the tiller almost up to your ear as you try to keep the boat going in a straight line. But a scow will sail along, heel right up, and capsize, and there will hardly be any change in tiller pressure. A scow can heel over and dump you in the creek with hardly a clue from the tiller that things are going wrong! So you soon learn about a lot of things that go beyond just the pressure on the helm when you're sailing a scow. You'll quickly learn that you had better start to think about dropping your travelers and easing your mainsail as soon as you begin to heel over too far. If you don't, you are going to be upside down in the middle of the course, and your race will be over.

A keelboat will usually give you an out by going hard-to-wind for a moment, and all you have lost in the process will be a couple of boat lengths. But a keelboat will also let you get away with *not* doing certain things, which can make you a bit careless. And that is why I think so many sailors who have learned on centerboard boats—particularly the kind that are sailed on the lakes of the Midwest—have been able to go on and sail other boats with a great deal of success. The major reason is that these sailors are very conscious of the proper amount of heel a boat should have and they know what steps to take when things start to get a little bit out of control.

Don't think for a minute that a new boat or new equipment will save you from a poor start or work you up to first place at the windward mark. At the top level of boat-for-boat racing, equipment simply isn't a key factor. A friend of mine had an older boat that he had worked on and had brought up to racing standard. He had the boat for three years and had done very well racing it. In the fourth year he bought a brand new boat—and his race results went all to pot. He *knew* that his old boat was not quite equal to the rest, so he practiced very hard, was very careful about how his sails were set up, and put a lot of thought into everything he did when sailing. With the new boat, he didn't bother to practice because he assumed his new equipment would automatically give him an edge in speed; he didn't bother to develop a program of preparation. The result was that he finished the season below his average of the previous year. It happens all the time in sailboat racing; when you get complacent and assume you are going to do better, the chances are that just the reverse will happen.

So don't forget that any new boat that you leave sitting on the trailer or on a mooring is not going to help you win races; you have to go out and pound the water with it, learn its language, and listen to what it has to tell you.

PREPARING THE HULL

A boat that has a good racing finish improves your confidence, and that is crucial for serious competition. If you have a fiberglass boat with a gelcoat finish, and you are satisfied that the hull shape is correct and to the legal specifications, you should start to bring the finish of the hull up to racing standard. This is accomplished in only one way: sanding.

But first test the surface by slowly drawing your fingertips across the hull. Don't tense your fingers; just keep them under firm pressure as you slowly move your hand across the hull surface. As your fingers move across the finish, you will feel any ripples or imperfections in the gelcoat. You can start either from the sheer and pull your hand down, or begin from the keel and pull it up.

When you have located a spot that needs work, take a lead pencil (ink can stain the gelcoat) and mark, with a straight line, all the high spots that need to be sanded. Mark all the low points with a circle. Now take a piece of #320 wet/dry sandpaper and wrap it around a ½-inch Styrofoam block (Fig. 3-1). Fill a pail with water and add a mild liquid detergent. The soap keeps the sandpaper from clogging, and it cleans the hull surface.

When you are sanding, rub in a fore-and-aft direction; nev-

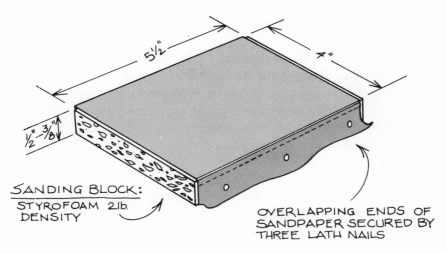

5½"

4"

½" – ³/₈"

SANDING BLOCK:
STYROFOAM 2lb.
DENSITY

OVERLAPPING ENDS OF
SANDPAPER SECURED BY
THREE LATH NAILS

Fig. 3-1. When you are working on the hull, use a sanding block of the sort shown here. Never use only your hand, for this will leave streaked indentations on the hull surface.

er go up and down. Keep the upper part of your body directly over your arm and elbow as you work. If you have a high spot, work it down; if you have a low spot, sand around the edges until the entire surface is even. When you have finished with the #320 paper, begin the entire process again with #400 wet/dry paper. Then complete the job with #500 paper, and finally #600 paper.

Use plenty of liquid soap and water, and don't think that just because you are moving to a finer-grit paper you can speed up the sanding process. You may spend two hours going down the side of a 20-foot boat with #400 paper. But if you only spend half an hour with #500, and half an hour with #600, you are going to have #400 scratches in your finish when you are all through.

Prepare the keel, centerboard, and rudder in exactly the same way. Start with #320 wet/dry sandpaper and work up through the grades to #600 finish. Never use any grade of sandpaper without a block, for you will leave finger streaks on the surface. The ½-inch flexible Styrofoam block forms to the hull nicely and allows it to bridge the highs and lows. Always try and make the intersecting corners of the transom as sharp as possible.

When you have finished with your #600 paper, you should apply rubbing compound to the hull and keel surfaces. Rub the compound in with a fore-and-aft motion using a soft cloth. Finish by burnishing the hull with another soft cloth. If you are preparing the boat for a regatta, take a sponge and apply pure liquid soap to the entire surface of the hull twelve to twenty-four hours before the boat is to go into the water and let it dry on the hull.

If class rules permit, you might even consider putting a Teflon spray coating underneath the soap but right on top of the hand-rubbed finish. Keep in mind that one session with rubbing compound won't get you through a season. After about a month of sailing think about giving the boat another rubdown with the compound.

There are a few things to avoid when preparing your hull: Do not use a mechanical polisher, because it creates microscopic waves on the hull. Disc or belt sanders should be avoided, because they can leave half-moons and gouges in a hull. Never use wax, because it builds up unevenly and slows your boatspeed through the water.

A good sanding and finishing job does take time. Two people who know what they are doing can spend two full days, or thirty-two hours, getting what I would consider a good speed finish on the hull of a 25-foot boat. But if you work carefully and smoothly, you will wind up with a beautifully finished hull. And the smoother the finish, the faster the boat—and the happier the skipper.

If you have a wooden boat, you've got to keep the water out of the wood. If you don't seal your boat, moisture will make the wood heavy; it will take forever to dry out the hull. You prevent this by using good paint. But you have to prepare the hull properly for painting, and that means proper sanding. Start out with #320. (Use #220 if the old varnish or paint surface is a little rough.) Then wipe the surface clean with a damp cloth and paint the hull. Let the paint sit untouched for about four weeks (enough time for the paint to cure). Now you can sand the hull with #600 paper, follow that up with rubbing compound, and finally apply liquid soap.

The traditional way to paint a small boat is to turn it upside down and paint it from the keel down. I think a better way is to hang a boat right side up from the overhead. This way you are sure to get a finish that is free from dust. (A good general tip for minimizing dust: keep the floor damp or even wet.)

If you keep your boat in the water, its bottom will be susceptible to marine growth, so you should apply a good antifouling paint. The bottom preparation here is about the same as it would be for a boat that is drysailed. Start with #320 wet/dry sandpaper. Then apply several coats of the paint of your choice. Let the paint cure, then sand the surface again, going up through the grades to #600 paper.

If you damage the hull or keel and need to make a repair, you should fill in the hole, smooth it, and gelcoat the surface. Then you can start out again with the #320 wet/dry sandpaper and work on up through the grades to the #600. Then go to your hand rub. If you have done everything correctly, your repaired finish should be identical to what you have on the rest of the boat.

I know there are people who say a slightly roughened surface finish is fast, but I don't believe it. For me the smoother the hull, the faster it is going to be. And on a fiberglass boat it is that hand rubbing and burnishing that is going to get it for you.

When you are traveling, take good care of your rudder and centerboard. Get some ¼-inch rubber foam and place a piece on either side of your centerboard and rudder. Then make a profile scabbard out of a tough material and slip both the blade and foam inside. Cover up an exposed keel in a similar way by making a scabbard and fitting it up over the keel section. The scabbard prevents sand or other debris from damaging the finish when you are on the road.

If you are competing in a major regatta, one of the things you might plan to do when you first get there is to give the boat another complete hand-rubbing, and follow that up with the liquid-soap treatment. This extra effort can work in two ways: First, no effort to prepare your boat is ever too great. And second, this kind of preparation is bound to be noticed by your competitors, and that can give you a psychological edge.

In the Olympics at Kiel, West Germany, I started to worry about the bottom of my Soling. I became so concerned that I told the crew they could do whatever they wanted to on the layday before the fifth race. But I wanted to make sure the boat was right, so I got it out of the water and hand-rubbed the entire hull by myself. Then I applied some Teflon spray and finished the job with the liquid soap. The next day we were ahead of everyone by two boat lengths at the first windward mark, and we had a quarter of a mile lead on everyone at the leeward mark. Who is to say my work the previous day hadn't helped?

The reason for all this preparation is to eliminate all your underwater hangups. You do this by finishing your hull with sandpaper and rubbing compound, and getting the condition of your blades at least equal to those of the fleet leaders. After all, if you are equal with your competition in these categories, you can beat them somewhere else: on the starting line, in sail shape, or in a maneuver.

Always try to do the sanding and rubbing yourself. If you don't have complete confidence in your hull and bottom preparation, the chances are good that you will be slower through the water. The problem may all be in your head, of course, but having a problem there is just as important to the outcome of a race as having an actual imperfection below the waterline!

DECK LAYOUTS

When I was starting out in the Soling, there were some very good sailors who had joined the class, and Bruce Goldsmith was one of the best. He was extremely fast in almost every condition. I can remember one regatta when we were both beating to windward and it was nip and tuck. He would get an overlap on us and then we would break it. But three times within a quarter of a mile I saw Rob Lansing, one of Bruce's crew, come off the rail and go into the boat to make an adjustment. I knew Bruce's boat was laid out so all the adjustment lines led to a tray at the front end of the cockpit. Every time Rob came off the rail we gained 3 or 4 feet. But we were both still fighting tooth and nail for the lead position.

Then I just reached down and eased off the line controlling the backstay. My hand had to ease out only about 3 inches of line which, when I calculate the mechanical advantage we had in the pulley system below decks, eased the backstay wire out just under half an inch. That easing of the backstay straightened the mast just enough to pull my mainsail leech up about an inch and a half. And with that increased hook in the main, we just walked up quickly to windward.

Once we were up where I wanted to be, I put my hand down on the control line again and pulled the backstay back in to bend the mast and reintroduce a high-speed shape in the mainsail. We immediately gained the controlling position.

That story pretty much describes my philosophy on deck layouts. There is no point in having something on a boat if you can't adjust it quickly and easily. And you shouldn't ever have to move around the boat (especially a small boat) to make an adjustment. All good deck layouts should use these rules as a philosophical starting point.

Also keep in mind that if you reach to make an adjustment, you grab that tail, and the tail doesn't move, that adjustment system ought to come off the boat. My reasoning here is that either the adjustment isn't any good in the first place or the mechanical advantage you have dreamed up is not sufficient. You must be able to tweak every string and have movement: the cunningham moves, the traveler drops, or the backstay, boom vang, or whatever goes in or out smoothly.

The distance you move the adjustment tail is directly proportional to the mechanical advantage you have devised. If, for example, the advantage is 2:1, you are going to have to pull something 2 inches to get the adjustment to move 1 inch. A Soling boom vang can have an 18:1 mechanical advantage, which means that for every 18 inches of pull you get 1 inch of adjustment.

How you lay out all your controls on a boat is important, but equally important is the crew you anticipate sailing with. For example, if you have three in the crew and you know the person closest to the bow is an excellent sail setter, you should set things up so that this crew member has the outhaul adjustment within easy reach and is in charge of making the decisions on the mainsail.

A poorly engineered deck layout will certainly create problems. If the mechanical advantage is so poor that when a skipper or crew member of average strength grabs a line, pulls it, and gets no reaction, the only thing that has happened is that somebody's head and body have been thrown back out of the racing position—and the line hasn't even been moved. And if you are the one trying to make the adjustment, you now have two problems: you are off balance, and the jolt has broken your concentration; because you haven't been able to make the adjustment, you may have lost as much as two or three boat lengths to another boat that *has* been able to adjust.

If your nearest competitor happens to be in a position where 6 feet can make the difference between establishing a safe leeward position or having that boat run over you to windward and force you to do something you don't want to do, there is only one possible solution. Make sure your control adjustments are located within easy reach of everyone. Make sure the controls can be worked from both sides of the boat, and design all the mechanical systems so that you have enough mechanical advantage for each control and you can make an adjustment easily, no matter what the load on the system may be. Most of the time the reason something does not work is that friction has built up somewhere. To prevent this from happening, install only the best ball-bearing blocks and make sure they can carry the anticipated loads.

On a small boat I lead the controls that involve the speed adjustments (sails and traveler) to a spot where I can reach them with my forward hand as I sit on the windward side of the boat. It is a great comfort to be able to reach down, pull on something, and get a reaction without having to bother the rest of the crew with a discussion on what to take in, and how much. On bigger boats, the middle crew can join me on the keyboard, playing the adjustment tunes with his aft hand.

Visibility, in addition to position and mechanical advantage, is an important factor in every deck layout. For example, when I am sailing to windward I concentrate on the waves and the wind and I don't ever take my eyes off what's ahead of me to look up at my sails. If I want to hook my boat up to windward and get clear of a boat that is down below, I might ease my backstay control just a bit. I don't have to look at the sail because I know that when I ease that backstay control line the mast is going to straighten up a little from its bent position, and because of this the batten section is going to hook up to windward as the sail takes on a little more camber. Now I can start to point up a little higher and get away from the boat below me. But the important point is that I can do all this without having to look at either the sail or the deck. I can continue to look straight ahead and concentrate on those waves and the way the boat is moving through the water.

Once I am far enough to windward so I have the distance I need to prevent the boat to leeward from getting control over me, I just reach down and take up on my backstay again. I put bend back in the mast, reflatten my sail for straight-line sailing, and drive over the top of my competitor. And throughout the entire procedure I haven't had to look anywhere except straight ahead.

You will be performing these kinds of maneuvers often during a race. It's very much like shifting down on the curves in a race car, then speeding up again when you get on the straightaway. The backstay, vang, cunningham, and traveler all are part of the gearshifting maneuvers, and it is important to be able to adjust as many of them as possible without having to look at the adjustment. The corollary, of course, is that you must be able to visualize what is taking place with the mainsail or jib shape as you make that adjustment and do so without taking your eyes off what is up ahead of you.

You should know what kind of sails to put on your boat and

know how much they are going to like, or dislike, being adjusted. For example, if you are planning to use a mainsail that has been designed so it doesn't require much mast bend, you are wasting your time putting an 18:1 backstay adjuster on the boat when a 4:1 system will do just as well. But if your mainsail is designed for a lot of mast bend—possibly as much as 2 feet—you must have a potent mechanical advantage on the backstay, or some windy day you are going to be standing right up in the boat flexing your legs, back, and arm muscles to get that backstay in. Your ability to concentrate on your steering, of course, is completely lost.

So always plan your deck layouts to match the flexibility needs of your sails. Never put on more controls than you need. But don't underestimate the possible power requirements when you are assessing what mechanical advantages to put on a particular lead.

Say a boat tacks right on top of you and you have to drop down 5 or 10 yards below your straight-line course to get clear of the other boat's wind shadow. If you break off to leeward without dropping your travelers, your boat becomes overpowered, heels over, and your rudder drag builds up as you try to fight the helm. But if you can maintain the same angle of heel with just a slight easing of the jib sheet and main traveler controls, you can power away from the other boat with ease. This is the true value of a well-laid-out sail and rig control system. If your deck controls can't accomplish this kind of maneuver, you will always be beaten, no matter how well you may sail the rest of the race.

If you are confused about what controls to install, one easy way to learn what works is to take a close look at the layouts of the leaders in the fleet. The chances are excellent those crews have spent a lot of time thinking about all the potential problems, and their solutions should cut many hours of trial-and-error off your own time.

Controls are always going to differ slightly from one boat to another, but don't lose sight of what the controls are supposed to do. They are there to help you power your boat over a racecourse, particularly at the corners, or turning marks. A successful control reacts to fingertip touch; that is, it enables you to keep your concentration focused on a good mark-rounding or getting yourself into a good offensive or defensive position relative to the boats around you. Spend a good deal of time designing your deck layout—you simply can't afford a poorly designed lead for any of your mast and sail adjustments.

MAST AND RIGGING

The first thing to do is look closely at the masts used by the top three sailors in the fleet; get the same mast if that seems to be a reasonable solution. If you disagree with them, make sure you have some very good reasons for doing so. Selecting a mast is fairly easy in a one-design class, but if you are involved in offshore racing, talk to a designer before you jump in with something no one else is using.

But no matter what type of boat you sail, there are several fundamentals to keep in mind. If your shrouds or control wires don't extend all the way to the top of the mast, make sure the mast and its tip can support the leech of the mainsail in all the wind and sea conditions you expect to be sailing in. Conditions do vary, of course, and you can get by with a softer mast section if you are going to be doing a lot of flat-water sailing. You will need a much stiffer section if you want to be successful in windy and choppy conditions, where you need additional strength from the mast.

If you have a boat that sails best with very little heel, as most dinghies do, you don't have to get very excited about the weight of the mast tip. But on a keelboat like a Star, it is very important to have a tip that is light but that can also carry the leech of the mainsail without having the sail go soft and collapse every time the boat hits a wave. This is one area where I don't think you should argue with what the leaders have selected unless you really have a good reason for doing so.

There is a long-standing debate regarding the benefits of stiff spars as opposed to flexible ones. The Flying Dutchman, for example, has gone, over the years, from a flexible mast to a stiff one and back to flexible. My feeling is that if you sail a reasonably high-performance boat that carries a flat mainsail shape in light air, you are better off if you have a flexible spar.

Anodizing your spar section puts the most durable finish you can get on the mast. The finish is highly scratch-resistant and is tolerant of salt water. A painted finish is not as desirable for racing because paint doesn't penetrate the section and thus is vulnerable to surface chipping and scratching. It is also a good idea to hand-rub your spar with rubbing compound before any major regatta. And you can follow that by applying some good paste wax to the mast so it will shed any impurities (like sea-spray) that might try to attach themselves to the surface.

Always check your mast and rigging before every practice session or race. Look at the shroud mounts, tangs, spreader tips, and spreader roots. Even though stainless steel is fairly resistant to fatigue, every now and then I find a tang that has a crack. Never drill more holes than you need in the mast section, because this will weaken it. If you want to cover a hole, use a piece of smooth tape. Holes that you leave uncovered do disturb the airflow over the mast.

When the season is over, wipe down all your rigging with an oily cloth before you put it away. (Vaseline spread on a rubber glove is another good method.) You can wipe the rigging clean again in the spring. Lubricate all moving parts regularly during the sailing season, and if you have a wire halyard that runs over a nonmoving part, or through a stainless-steel tube, rub beeswax into the halyard at least once a month (or every two weeks if you are sailing a lot). Any halyard that does not run over a rotating surface like a sheave will gall fairly quickly. Beeswax in the lay of the halyard makes it run just as smoothly as it would if it were going over a wheel or sheave.

Despite the claim that aerodynamics are not critical in sailing because sailboats travel at slow speeds, having a clean mast and rig that is free of bumps and extrusions is important. Keeping all the bumps to a minimum certainly can't hurt.

And here again, if you know you have a superior finish on your spar, it will set your mind at ease and give you a sense of well-being. So the extra time you spend on your mast is well worth the effort.

Mast Tune

You should understand the basic principles of mast tune, so you have an idea about what is going to affect your spar in different conditions. If you are sailing a fractional rig with a partially unsupported upper section, the ideal light-air mast configuration is with the head of the mainsail directly over the tack. You don't want the tip of the mast leaning off to leeward, for this reduces sail power. In order to get the tip to stand up like this, let the mast have a very shallow sag to leeward below the spot where the shrouds intersect. You want to have maximum sag right at the point where the spreaders intersect the mast, and you create this sag by easing off the lower shrouds. This sag to leeward starts the mast section, above the shroud intersection point, angling to windward. This windward angle is what permits the unsupported tip of the mast to become positioned right over the tack. This midsection sag to leeward is the sort of configuration to strive for when winds are under about 12 knots, or any time you want to get maximum power from your sail.

A heavy-air situation, where you are overpowered, calls for the opposite mast configuration. To get it you tighten the lower shrouds and keep the middle section at the spreaders straight. Now the tip is able to fall off to leeward, and this depowers the mainsail. It also opens up the slot area between the leech of the jib and the main. In general this is the way you ought to set up a fractional rig when winds exceed 12 to 15 knots (Fig. 3-2).

Spreaders play a key role in all partially supported masts. In many boats the spreaders are swept back to produce additional support for the headstay load. This type of rig is quite common; you see it on any boat that carries a large headsail. However, swept-back spreaders produce a "softer" rig, and the mast section below the headstay attachment point might

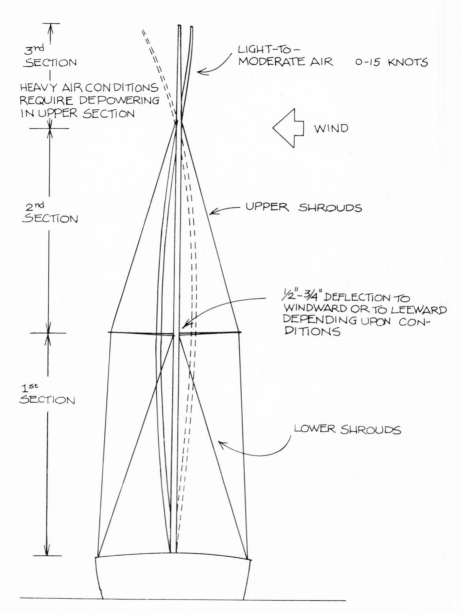

3rd
SECTION

HEAVY AIR CONDITIONS
REQUIRE DEPOWERING
IN UPPER SECTION

LIGHT–To–
MODERATE AIR   0-15 KNOTS

WIND

2nd
SECTION

UPPER SHROUDS

½"-¾" DEFLECTION TO
WINDWARD OR TO LEEWARD
DEPENDING UPON CON-
DITIONS

1st
SECTION

LOWER SHROUDS

Fig. 3-2. An exaggerated view of a mast, showing a three-section sag. To keep
the mast tip over the base for moderate wind conditions, ease the lower
shrouds to let the section sag to leeward at the spreaders. For heavy air, ease
the upper shrouds to let the section deflect to windward at the spreaders. The
tip falls off to leeward and depowers the sail.

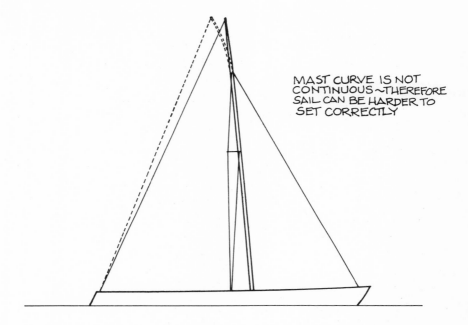

MAST CURVE IS NOT
CONTINUOUS ~THEREFORE
SAIL CAN BE HARDER TO
SET CORRECTLY

Fig. 3-3. Swept-back spreaders are a good configuration for any boat that requires a significant headstay load. However, in the lower section the mast curvature will not be constant and this makes it more difficult to set a mainsail.

tend to flex forward when you take up hard on the headstay (Fig. 3-3).

And swept-back spreaders make it difficult to get a good continuous curve along the lower two-thirds of the spar. The good part of all this is that this type of rig can support a heavy headstay load with relative ease.

A fixed spreader rig usually has the spreaders set at about 90 degrees to the mast, with the shroud bases in line with the mast. In fact on a Soling rig, the spreaders are angled just a bit forward of 90 degrees, and this is what makes the center section of the mast so stiff compared to the swept-back spreader configuration. When these shrouds are tightened, the mast is actually driven aft at the spreader base, which makes the middle of the mast, with no headstay tension, deflect slightly toward the stern. Here again, the final curve

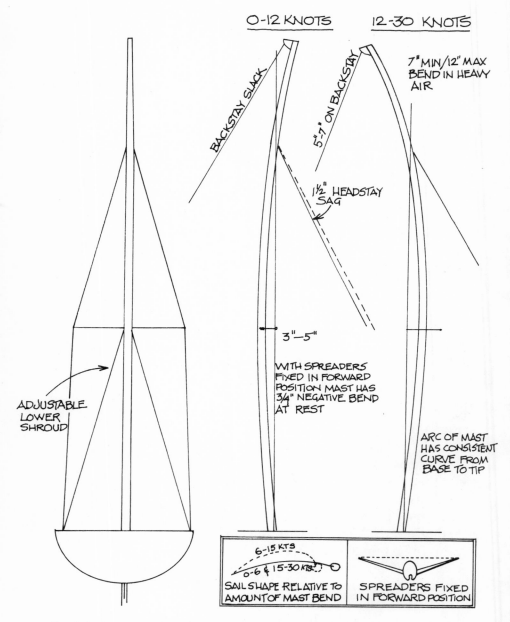

0-12 KNOTS

12-30 KNOTS

BACKSTAY SLACK

5"-7" ON BACKSTAY

7" MIN/12" MAX BEND IN HEAVY AIR

1½" HEADSTAY SAG

3"—5"

WITH SPREADERS FIXED IN FORWARD POSITION MAST HAS ¾" NEGATIVE BEND AT REST

ARC OF MAST HAS CONSISTENT CURVE FROM BASE TO TIP

ADJUSTABLE LOWER SHROUD

6-15 KTS

0-6 & 15-30 KTS

SAIL SHAPE RELATIVE TO AMOUNT OF MAST BEND

SPREADERS FIXED IN FORWARD POSITION

Fig. 3-4. A mast with its spreaders fixed in a forward position can create a smooth mast bend in the tensioned position. One big advantage of this type of rig is that headstay tension can be varied to adapt to different wind strengths.

of the mast is determined by the way you tension your shrouds (Fig. 3-4).

Remember, though, that the amount of fore-and-aft curve you put into your mast must be related carefully to the design of your mainsail. If you are going to have a versatile sail that can set well over a wide range of conditions, the luff curve and mast curve have to be closely coordinated.

Finally, a fully supported section with a shroud that runs up to the mast tip (as in the Star) gets its control, in the athwartship direction, from the intermediate shroud. Star sailors also like a slight deflection to leeward in the midsection of the mast, and they get it by slacking both the intermediate and the lower shroud to get a smooth sag that runs from the heel of the mast to the tip (Fig. 3-5).

Backstay tension affects the curvature of the mast, but increased backstay tension also reduces jib luff sag. While there is nothing basically wrong with this, you do have to be

Fig. 3-5. A typical Star mast section shows how the deflection can be varied by easing both the lower and intermediate shrouds.

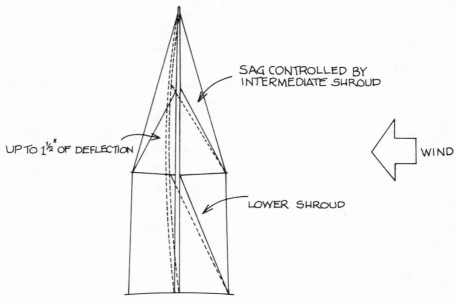

SAG CONTROLLED BY INTERMEDIATE SHROUD

UP TO 1½" OF DEFLECTION

WIND

LOWER SHROUD

aware of what is happening in this relationship, and here again it is important that you try to set your rig up so that your jib luff sag and the fore-and-aft mast curve are coordinated with the sails you plan on using.

If the rig on your boat has a constantly rigid headstay, you probably will need several different jibs instead of a single jib whose camber you can control by adjusting the amount of headstay sag. A rigid headstay system is very common on offshore racing boats, and it works fine—just as long as you are able to make all the necessary sail changes when weather conditions dictate. But on a small boat you really don't have that option; that is why you should assess the potential for tuning your headstay and your mast camber to your sails so they can all work together.

For the most part, dinghy masts are stepped through the deck, and you control the fore-and-aft bend at the mast partners. Whether a dinghy spar works properly as far as athwartships bend is concerned depends on the length of the spreader and the angle at which the spreaders are fixed. If you mount the long spreaders that can swing in a fore-and-aft direction, when a load starts to build up to the windward shroud the middle part of the mast begins to bend forward and to leeward. When this happens the tip of the mast falls off to leeward. This lateral deflection is a good configuration to have when you are sailing in very light air, and when you are in heavy winds of 15 knots or more. It is good in light air because the luff of the mainsail moves further to windward. This opens up the slot between jib and main, and the increased slot area helps you point to windward more efficiently in light air. In heavy winds, the deflection of the tip to leeward depowers the mainsail and reduces the heeling forces on the boat. Between the very light and very heavy wind conditions, you can fix the spreaders to keep the mast in line and give you good power and support for the mainsail leech. Fixed spreaders also keep the width of the slot at the proper distance and depth for the normal range of wind conditions (Fig. 3-6).

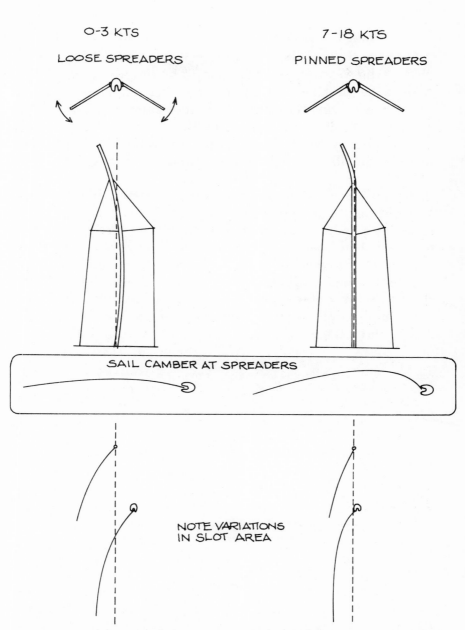

0-3 KTS

LOOSE SPREADERS

7-18 KTS

PINNED SPREADERS

SAIL CAMBER AT SPREADERS

NOTE VARIATIONS
IN SLOT AREA

Fig. 3-6. With dinghy masts, the position of the spreaders, and whether they are fixed or swinging, has a significant effect on mast deflection, sail shape, and the size of the slot area.

Mast Rake

On many types of boats, but especially on dinghies, you can change the sheeting point of your jib by simply changing the rake of the mast. Increasing mast rake has the same effect on your jib as moving the deck attachment point aft. Conversely, straightening the mast moves the theoretical trim point forward. In heavy winds you will probably want to open up the leech of the jib, and you do this by increasing mast rake (Fig. 3-7).

Raking the mast aft also means that the section lays off to leeward slightly as you sail to windward. This is another way to depower whenever you get in an overpowered condition on a heavy-air beat.

Finally, "slopping the rig," as it is called, is a further variation on the idea of getting the rig off to leeward. To understand this, think of the normal situation in which the wind hits your sailplan at 90 degrees. Obviously at this angle the maximum wind force is working on the rig and sails. But when you

Fig. 3-7. Mast rake helps the upper part of the jib twist off, and this frees the leech in heavier winds. Increasing rake has the same effect on the jib as moving its clew trim point aft.

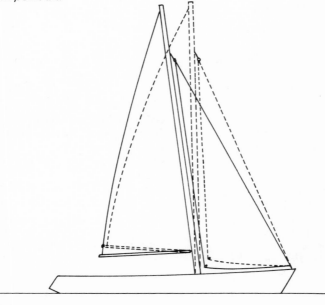

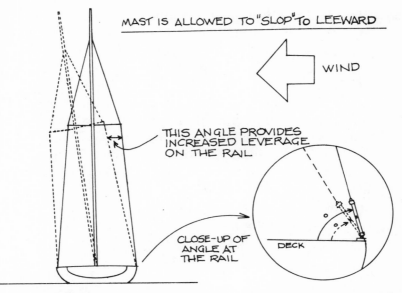

Fig. 3-8. If the design of the rig permits, easing the shrouds off lets the rig "slop" to leeward, which decreases the force of the wind on the rig. In heavy conditions this can improve performance dramatically by increasing the amount of leverage provided at the windward rail.

drop that angle down to 75 degrees, the force of the wind hitting the sail is reduced (Fig. 3-8). Iceboat rigs might be slopped as much as 3 feet to leeward at the tip of the mast. When this is done the boats immediately come back under control. In a conventional sailing situation you might only be talking about 18 inches of slop at the masthead, but the principle is exactly the same. You are, in effect, reducing the force of the wind to a point where you are not overpowered. You use the resulting force to maximize your straight-line speed through the water.

However if the rig has been slopped and the boat now is standing up too straight, there is a good chance that you are not making your best speed and therefore that you could be making excess leeway. But if you are clearly overpowered, think about reducing the wind's force on the rig by getting it to lie off to leeward. Once you have a wind force that is not trying to blow you over, you can increase your speed through the water. And that is when the rudder, and the centerboard or keel, bite in and start to give you maximum lift. That's when you can go to windward in an optimum mode.

One final reason to rake a rig aft is that the wind does leave the leech of the sail at an angle, and the closer that angle is to 90 degrees, the higher the speed potential is for that rig. Air flows off a sail in a fanning motion, spreading up over the top of the sail and down under the bottom of the boom. When winds are light to medium you want to present the maximum amount of sail area to the wind, and the mast should be as vertical as possible. But in heavier air, the closer the wind can be to that 90-degree angle as it flows off the leech, the more efficient the sail is going to be. Again we see this in iceboats, where there is a dramatic performance difference depending on the angle the iceboat sail makes to the wind. The more perpendicular the leech is to the flow, the better the performance (Fig. 3-9).

Fig. 3-9. Increasing mast rake improves the flow of air off the leech of the mainsail. The more leech area that is perpendicular to the flow, the more efficient the sail.

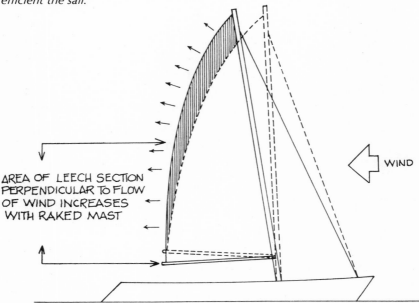

Every sail gets its driving force from its shape, and this power is controlled by the amount and location of a sail's draft, or camber. Never allow the air flow to stall or separate from the sail's surface (unless you become overpowered) because that reduces the driving force of the sail. Always keep in mind that it is the amount and the velocity of the air that flows across the underside of your sails that determine how much power you are going to get from those sails. Maintaining this smooth flow applies to all points of sail: on the wind as well as running free.

SAIL CONTROLS

The Proper Line

While it is true that the smaller a line's diameter, the more difficult it is to hold, a slender line is preferable for two reasons: first, it runs more easily over a pulley or sheave; and second, the smaller line makes it easier to tell what the sail is actually doing. A heavier and thicker line is easier to hold, but I guarantee it won't give you as much warning when a spinnaker is about to collapse as will a smaller line.

There are so many different kinds of line available today that it is difficult to make any specific recommendations on which type to get. I like to sail with the fuzzy spun-Dacron lines because they are less apt to slip through my hands. Kevlar lines are excellent for spinnaker sheets and guys because they are available in very small sizes and they don't stretch. This no-stretch characteristic is very important with a sail like a spinnaker, for you never want to have the spinnaker pole pumping back and forth as you go through waves. Any line that can stretch will do this to your spinnaker pole, and that can hurt your boatspeed.

How do you hold onto a small line? With hands that are toughened up! For one-design racing I make a special point to get my hands into condition very early in the season so I can use a diameter of line that is one size smaller than anyone else is using out on the course.

Backstay

Though the mainsheet and jibsheet are the primary means
you have to control the angle a sail makes to the wind, the
more subtle sail controls can be critical aids in getting the
right shape for the right conditions. Mast bend, as we have
seen, is a major element in getting the proper mainsail shape,
and on most boats the best way to control mast bend is with
the backstay. Dinghies and boats without backstays use boom-
vang tension to produce a bend in the mast.

Increasing backstay tension pulls the top of the mast aft.
This decreases the distance between the end of the boom and
the head of the sail; as a result, the batten section drops off to
leeward and depowers the mainsail. Conversely, easing off on
the backstay straightens the mast; the batten section then
stands up to compensate for the greater distance between the
end of the boom and the head of the sail. Any time you bend a
mast, the leech falls away to leeward; if you don't adjust other
things further, you will lose driving force and you will wind
up heading off dramatically to maintain your speed through
the water.

Outhaul

The outhaul controls the amount of camber in the lower
half of the mainsail; a tight outhaul flattens the forward, or
entry, section of the mainsail's lower half. When winds are
light or very heavy, a tight outhaul also helps increase the
width of the slot. You should ease the outhaul a bit in medium
winds, when a fuller mainsail shape works more effectively.

Halyard

Halyard tension controls the amount of draft in the top half
of a sail, the cunningham and downhaul control the draft in
the bottom half of the sail. However, you should know that
once a sail starts to become loaded up because of increased
wind pressure, the sail fabric starts to move down the spar.

You can prove this to yourself by standing on your boom
and putting a piece of tape on the mast as high as you can
reach. Now hoist the mainsail and mark the luff of the sail

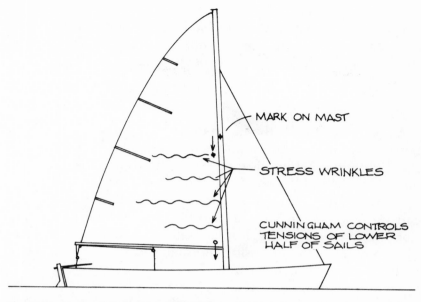

Fig. 3-10. As a sail loads up under increased wind pressure, the sail will move down the mast. This means halyard tension must be used to control the draft in the upper part of the sail, and cunningham tension applied to control the draft in the lower half of the sail.

next to the tape. As the wind comes up, the sail might move down as much as 4 to 6 inches on a boat with a 26-foot mast. This is where the cunningham control can help, by removing the stress wrinkles that form as the sail creeps down along the spar (Fig. 3-10).

Cunningham

The cunningham's basic function is to control the fore-and-aft location of the draft in the lower half of the sail. Tensioning the cunningham drives the draft forward in the sail. In fact, if you apply too much cunningham, you can drive the camber too far forward, creating a shape that produces no lift at all in the forward part of the sail. Remember, too, that the leech of the main will fall off whenever the cunningham is tensioned, and if you tighten it up too hard, you run the risk of tripping the leech and having it fall way off to leeward. This is another reason why you must be able to adjust all your sail controls quickly. If the wind suddenly drops from 18 knots or so to something under 10 knots, and you don't ease the cunningham right away, your leech is going to flop over to leeward like a dishrag.

Boom Vang

A boom vang holds the boom down, but it also affects leech tension. Tightening the vang decreases camber in the sail but this tightening action also increases the downward pressure on the leech, and the result can be a leech section that hooks up to windward. While there are a few conditions where you can use your boom vang as a substitute for mainsheet tension—in flat water, or high-speed sailing conditions, for example—you are better off using the mainsheet and the traveler to achieve good leech control.

Sailing on the wind in sloppy sea conditions, where you need maximum power from your sails, use your boom vang to hold the boom down. But also try to let the outer end of the boom float just a bit by not using too much mainsheet tension. If there is no downward pressure from the mainsheet, the batten section of the sail is able to breathe, and it can move in and out with a fanning motion as the boat sails over the waves. This ability to fan reduces the tendency of the boat to pitch up and down in the seas.

Let me explain this last point in more detail. When the bow lifts as it moves into a sea, the top of the mast moves aft in an arc, and the apparent wind at the top of the mast also moves aft. If the boom is able to rise a bit, the leech of the mainsail is free to float, and if the top of the sail has some twist in it, the upper leech section starts to open up. It fills and gives lift and drive to that part of the sail. This forward drive in turn helps resist the masthead movement toward the stern that has been created by the lifting bow. When the bow pitches forward down the back of the wave, the masthead moves forward and the apparent wind at the top of the mast also moves forward. Now, because of the twist, the top of the sail becomes stalled, with no driving power in the upper part of the sail. This

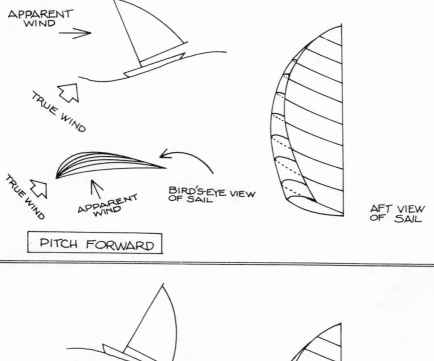

APPARENT WIND

TRUE WIND

TRUE WIND

APPARENT WIND

BIRD'S-EYE VIEW OF SAIL

AFT VIEW OF SAIL

PITCH FORWARD

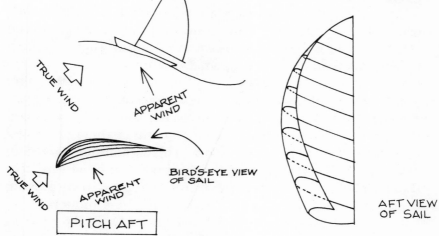

TRUE WIND

APPARENT WIND

TRUE WIND

APPARENT WIND

BIRD'S-EYE VIEW OF SAIL

AFT VIEW OF SAIL

PITCH AFT

Fig. 3-11. In conditions of light air and choppy sea, having a lot of twist in the upper part of the mainsail and jib reduces the tendency of the boat to pitch. The upper part of the sail stalls out as the mast pitches forward, reducing drive, but it develops power when the mast comes back and helps slow the rearward motion of the mast.

stalling cuts off the mainsail's driving power at the top of the mast; as a result there is no force to drive that part of the mast forward (Fig. 3-11).

The result of having a sail shaped so that it produces power up high as the mast whips aft, and stalls as it pitches forward, is that the pitching tendency of a boat is reduced considerably. If you use only your mainsheet to control the sail, inevitably there is a lot of downward pressure on the sail and you wind up with a leech that has no twist. As you power off the top of a wave, if you have a flat section up high, it will only accentuate the forward pitching motion. As the mast and sail come aft, the sail is going to stall because there is no offsetting power in the upper section of the sail to slow the rearward motion. The result is that the natural pitching motion becomes even worse.

However, if you have enough twist so the leech can float, the stalling that occurs when the mast pitches forward, and the power that comes on when the mast whips back are going to counteract these forces. This is the configuration you want to have when you are beating to windward in disturbed water. If you set your mainsail up properly, very often you can leave the rest of your competitors sitting there bobbing up and down and wondering what is wrong.

There is a small windsheer effect on all boats, with the wind speed increasing somewhat as you move up and away from the friction created at the surface of the water. This reduced friction makes the apparent wind a bit farther aft at the masthead than it is down below. This is another reason to have some twist in your sails, though I rarely use twist to solve this problem. I like twist primarily to keep my boat moving through the water with a minimum of pitching motion.

Jibs should also have a certain amount of twist; they should be trimmed so that the sail stalls whenever the bow pitches forward, and delivers maximum driving power when the bow lifts up on a wave.

Traveler
When you are sailing to windward, your most important

control is the traveler. It is the one adjustment device that doesn't seem to get half as much use as it should. A traveler can steer a boat to windward as effectively as a rudder, but it doesn't create drag in the water the way turning the rudder does.

Adjusting the traveler is also the best way to control a boat's heel angle once the proper mainsail shape has been established. If you become overpowered, the first thing to do is to ease off the main traveler, as well as the jib traveler if you have one. Dropping only the main traveler to leeward could force air coming off the jib onto the back of the mainsail, and usually this creates tremendous backwind on the main which destroys the flow over the forward part of the sail. So set your sail controls up so you can drop the jib clew down to leeward at the same time you ease the main traveler. Here is another case where you must think about how your adjustment controls are going to be set up. If you can't ease your travelers off and get them back up again quickly, you break your concentration—and that lapse in concentration is all it takes to throw you off and you will lose ground to a competitor.

The same sail-control principles apply to a masthead rig, though the headsail on these boats provides most of the driving force to windward. If you start to get overpowered, you cannot drop the jib down to leeward much. Instead you should shorten down quickly by going to a smaller headsail.

Mainsheet

The mainsheet determines how much twist there will be in the mainsail. And even though the mainsheet and traveler working together control the mainsail position, you should always drop the traveler down first if the wind comes up suddenly. If that isn't enough to bring the boat back up, then consider easing the main sheet.

In designing your deck layout, make sure that all sail adjustments can be made without ever having to look either at the sails or at another boat. You just can't afford to take your eyes off the wind and waves ahead. But if you start to heel 2 degrees and you don't adjust to stop that 2-degree heel, you have lost the opportunity to make distance to windward by heading up just enough to keep your angle of heel constant. If your boat starts to heel further, it is going to fall off its sailing lines, and then you'll start to lose speed over the bottom. But when you can make all these adjustments quickly with just a small movement of your hand, you won't have to worry about giving anything away to your competitors.

MAINSAIL

What is the ideal mainsail shape? The answer is that there is only one correct sail shape for any one set of conditions. But these conditions are constantly changing as the wind increases or decreases. And the condition of the water surface also changes with the rise and fall of the wind; this will also affect sail shape.

A good way to grasp the principles of sail shape is to think of the wing of an airplane. When the plane is flying along at a steady altitude, the flaps on the wing are trimmed in for speed and the wing's shape is relatively flat with a minimum amount of camber. But when the plane is either taking off or landing, the flaps are down and there is plenty of power being generated from those lifting surfaces to keep the aircraft airborne at the lower maneuvering speeds.

This, I think, is a good way to approach the setting up of your own sails. When you are just powering off a starting line, or when you need maximum power and drive (when you are sailing into heavy waves or slop, for example), you want to have enough power coming from your sails to keep you going. And that is when you want to have your "flaps"—the section at the luff and the leech of the sail—working to increase the camber and give you the speed you need for "takeoff" (Fig. 3-12).

To sail well you must know what a good sail shape is and also know how to use your control adjustments to get that shape. Probably the best way to learn what the basic shape should be is to go out sailing with the wind blowing around 12 knots. Put the boat on a close-hauled course, look at the shape

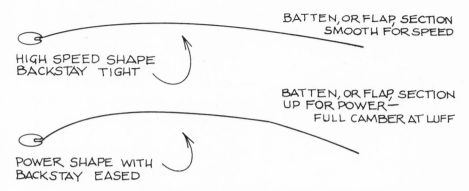

BATTEN, OR FLAP, SECTION
SMOOTH FOR SPEED

HIGH SPEED SHAPE
BACKSTAY TIGHT

BATTEN, OR FLAP, SECTION
UP FOR POWER—
FULL CAMBER AT LUFF

POWER SHAPE WITH
BACKSTAY EASED

Fig. 3-12. To change quickly from a high-speed sail shape to a power shape, ease the backstay to get the leech to hook up to windward and the luff to fill out.

in the sails, and commit that shape to memory. These are what I consider ideal sailing conditions; 12 knots of wind is enough to enable most boats to sail at their best. Once you have that basic foil shape clearly fixed in your mind, you should return to it any time you start to get confused.

When you are sailing on the wind for a period of time, you must continually change the shape of your sails and their angle of attack to the wind. Nothing is constant; the wind will come up or go down, the wave action is going to vary. All these things require action from you to keep the sails working at their maximum efficiency.

The first thing you should do is to check your leech, and this means checking your batten section. Start with the top batten and make sure it is parallel to the boom. The best way to check this is to get right underneath the boom and sight up over the windward side of the boom. If the top batten remains parallel to the boom, you are going to be right more times than you will be wrong when it comes to getting the correct sail shape.

For many years everyone thought you needed a flat mainsail for heavy weather, and another full-cut main that would "catch more wind" to use in the lighter stuff. With today's flexible masts and control systems, this rule no longer applies, and what now seems to work best is a sail whose section profile goes from being flat in the light wind to full in medium, and then to flat again in the heavy weather. In light air of 6 knots and under, you want to have a flat mainsail because this is the most efficient foil section for low wind speeds. You also want to have the slot between the jib and main opened up a bit; the best way to do this is to move the jib leads outboard.

As the wind builds up over 6 knots, you should start closing up the slot by increasing the camber in the mainsail to give it a fuller power shape, and also begin to move the jib leads inboard. You can keep this full power shape in both sails until the wind gets up to about 12 to 15 knots, at which point you probably are beginning to get overpowered and the boat is starting to heel over beyond its optimum heel angle. The precise wind speed where this happens varies a great deal, depending mostly on things like boat type and the weight of the crew.

As the wind speed moves up into this range, your boatspeed through the water also increases; the result is that now you can sail on a higher heading to the wind. And this, by itself, relieves some of the heeling pressure you get from a fuller sail. You should also counteract the increased pressure on the sails by getting the crew up on the windward rail. But eventually you will find that as the true wind starts blowing much over 12 knots, even with the crew on the rail, you will start to be overpowered. That's the time you must start flattening out your sail shapes again so that the large amount of lift developed by a full-shaped sail won't be wasted trying to push the mast of the boat over into the water!

In the higher wind ranges you want a sail shape that is fairly flat at the entrance of the sail, flat through the center and body of the sail, with a gentle tailing off of the batten section at the leech (Fig. 3-13). If you have to depower the mainsail in a gust, for example, the top batten gives you a good clue. If the top batten is falling off to leeward of the boom, you are depowering the sail. In a very strong wind, you might make the batten angle below the boom as much as 10 degrees. But

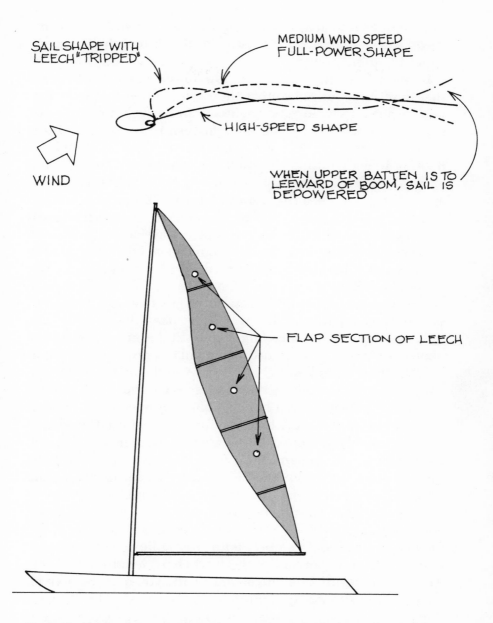

SAIL SHAPE WITH
LEECH "TRIPPED"

MEDIUM WIND SPEED
FULL-POWER SHAPE

HIGH-SPEED SHAPE

WHEN UPPER BATTEN IS TO
LEEWARD OF BOOM, SAIL IS
DEPOWERED

WIND

FLAP SECTION OF LEECH

Fig. 3-13. The leech area is where the controls are for both speed and power sailing. A slight turn of the batten section to windward is slightly slower, but it increases the options available to the helmsman when sailing to windward through waves.

even though you are depowering the sail, the increased wind speed keeps your total lift force relatively constant, so you won't be losing power.

In medium winds, however (up to about 12 knots), you should set up your sail so that the leech section makes a very gentle curve to windward; maintain a relatively full curve in the middle part of the sail. A slight turn to windward of the batten section can often keep your boat at the proper angle of heel as it goes into a confused sea condition. Though this curve does increase weather helm a little bit, if you misjudge an oncoming wave, a slight inward turn of the batten section increases your chances of correcting quickly and getting back on course. Of course, the more adept you are on the helm, the less hook to windward you are going to need in the batten section, and that is to be preferred, for any curve does slow your speed slightly.

The amount of shape you can put into a mainsail with your sail controls depends on the way it has been designed by the sailmaker. Generally speaking, a flat sail designed to have an open leech is easier to adjust than a sail designed with a fuller shape forward and a tight leech. A full-cut sail must be watched very carefully as the wind goes up and down.

Avoid having a sail that has only one "top speed" shape. For example, a sail that has a lot of draft designed into it produces a situation where you can't bend the mast much without having the leech collapse and fall off to leeward. Typically this sail has a fair amount of luff curve, which means it can perform well in only one particular set of conditions.

So get a sail that can be adjusted for a variety of wind conditions. While there is no set rule on the ideal location of maximum draft and camber, both should lie somewhere between 30 and 50 percent of the total chord length of the sail. And remember that when you are racing you must be able to change your sail shape as often as necessary. On the starting line, for example, you want a full power section in your mainsail with a large camber forward and a fairly closed, or tight, leech aft. Fullness forward gives you the ability to accelerate, while the tight leech aft, with battens hooked up slightly, gives you the freedom to sail your boat high on the wind and protect yourself from any boats that might be coming up at you from underneath. The starting line is where you want your sail to be like that airplane wing at takeoff: with its flaps in position for maximum lift.

Then, during the first minute or so of the race, you want to pull away from the rest of the pack by accelerating quickly. You do this by keeping as much camber in the sail as you can for the given wind conditions. After the minute has gone by, or whenever you have clear air, start working on your sail to get it to assume the flatter, more desirable, high-speed shape.

Now if someone comes in and clamps what is called a safe leeward position on you, that boat now has the same relationship to your boat as your jib has to your mainsail. Getting a safe leeward is a good offensive strategy, but unlike the beneficial effect of such a flow over your own jib and mainsail, you have to get yourself out of that spot immediately, because both the quarter wave and the bad air generated by the other boat are now affecting you. Instead of tacking away, this is the time to increase your camber in the mainsail and pull your batten section to windward. With this additional camber you can climb up to windward away from the influence of the other boat. Then, once you are high enough, you can resume your straight-line sailing by reshaping the sail to its high-speed shape.

In many cases you can get the batten section up just by pulling the traveler up and creating a little bite. The resulting heel of the boat lets you work it to windward without using additional helm. However, if the traveler already is down to leeward 8 inches or more and there is a fresh breeze, pulling it up will only slow you down. This is where the sail would benefit from adjustments in the vang, sheet, and backstay tension. Incidentally, I find that a traveler that is pinned on centerline always makes a boat cranky when sailing to windward in any kind of sea condition. It is much better to set it to leeward at least several inches and possibly a great deal more, though it depends on the type of boat you are sailing.

JIB

One of the most important elements of good boatspeed to windward is timing the leech of the jib with the shape of the mainsail. This is what keeps the slot area working most efficiently. The idea is to set both sails up so the curve of the leech of the jib matches the curve made by the underside of the mainsail. Because the head of the jib does intersect the main at a point above the deck, the constantly decreasing space going up to that point must be compensated for. Usually this is done by designing a certain amount of twist into the top sections of the jib. But even so you must be constantly alert to maintaining this relationship and keeping the two sails parallel to each other in the slot area.

One way to keep the jib leech in tune with the mainsail is to put stripes, in a contrasting color, one inch apart on the underside of the spreader. Then you can install a window in the mainsail at spreader height so you can see the leeward spreader from your position on deck and you can tune the leech of the jib with the main.

This assumes you have set your mainsail and jib leads up correctly. If the mainsail is being continually backwinded by the jib, either the jib is not sheeted correctly or you have too much draft low in the mainsail. To get that draft out, increase the boom vang tension. This bends the spar down low, which should pull some of the draft out and eliminate the backwind.

If you look at your jib and you see the leech is cupping in, or it looks like a saucer instead of a streamlined foil, try moving your jib leads outboard and aft. This reduces the downward tension on the leech of the jib, and the hooking problem should be solved.

Tuning the jib with the main is one thing; proper jib trim is another. For example, you might think that if you start to have weather helm and the boat wants to turn into the wind, trimming the jib in more will help push the bow off the wind and thereby balance the boat. But that is not what happens. When you trim in the jib, the slot becomes more constricted and this *increases* rather than decreases your weather helm.

The reason is that the normal flow across the underside of the mainsail now is disturbed and this, in turn, reduces the amount of lift the main can develop.

Whenever you get into a sailing situation where you are confused about what is going on, always ease your jib out a little before you do anything else. Try easing your jib rather than pulling it in and see if you can't get a little more life flowing through that slot.

Always be aware of the traditional relationship between the center of effort of the sail plan and the center of lateral resistance of the hull. In a very well-balanced boat, you can change your helm by simply moving the location of the draft in the mainsail.

The more common way to change helm balance, though, is to rake the mast aft and move the sailplan back just a bit to build in a little more weather helm. Conversely, raking the mast forward will decrease weather helm. If you are in a dinghy, and you have too much helm, pull the centerboard aft enough to move the center of lateral resistance back; this should help balance the boat.

SPINNAKERS

There are many different cuts of spinnaker, the most common being the crosscut, radial-head, starcut, and triradial. Starcuts and triradials excel in close-reaching conditions because they are designed and built so they won't change their shape. But a triradial sail can be what is called a "condition" sail; that kind of flexibility is what you need in one-design sailing. The wider the wind range a spinnaker has, the better it is going to work for you. If you are limited in the number of spinnakers you can have aboard in a race, you definitely have to factor that in. If you are limited to one spinnaker, you want it to be an all-purpose sail. Though it does depend on the wind conditions, a triradial spinnaker might well be the cut for you, though a crosscut sail could also be very effective.

A small spinnaker is going to be lighter, and if it is cut relatively flat this sail can often be much more effective in light to medium air. In fact, a small spinnaker often beats the pants off a much larger running spinnaker that may look as though its total sail area can cover the waterfront. The reason is that the small sail weighs less and therefore can support itself in less wind and hang out there to create a viable shape. And because the shape is floating up there, the flat-cut spinnaker works much more efficiently than a full-cut sail; this is what gives it its efficiency in the light going even though it may be much smaller.

A small, flat reaching sail is apt to be very fast from 0 to about 8 knots of wind. Then, as you go up to the 10-to-12-knot range, the efficiency of the flat sail is matched and passed by a fuller sail. The bigger draft in the full-cut sail begins to develop its own power. As you get up over 12 knots a full-cut spinnaker definitely lets you sail faster off the wind, and this lets you open up your angles and sail more downwind than would be the case if you set the smaller, less powerful sail.

But as you get up to 18 to 20 knots of wind, the smaller sail once again becomes more effective than the fuller sail. So the efficiency curves for the flat and the full-cut spinnaker cross twice: once in the lower wind speeds and again up in the higher ranges. This means that if you are sailing in predominately light conditions, a full downwind running sail probably won't work half as well for you as a smaller and flatter spinnaker.

Successful downwind sailing, of course, requires good spinnaker work. In light air you are trying to fool Mother Nature by making the flow of wind over the sails greater than it actually is. You do this by heading up, onto the wind, to increase the flow of apparent wind across the sails. Then, as your boatspeed builds up and the apparent wind angle starts to move toward the bow of the boat, you can head off again, away from the wind, without easing the sails.

You keep the apparent wind at the same angle, but now you can sail further off the wind and more toward your objective. And you are moving faster through the water because of an apparent wind over the sails that you have, in a sense, created yourself. If you are aware of this and know how to keep your sails properly "ventilated" in this manner, you can sail in almost the same direction downwind as a boat that may have gone around a windward mark in light air, headed off immediately without building up any apparent wind first, and then sat dead in the water with the spinnaker hanging right down around its ears. The only difference is that you keep your apparent wind flowing over the sails—and that is what keeps a boat moving.

CENTERBOARD AND RUDDER

Always mark your centerboard so you know how far up or down it is. Once it's marked, you can change it for the different sailing conditions you will have to deal with. Never leave this adjustment to chance; always use known markings. This can give you great peace of mind about your adjustments, allowing you to think about more important things, like getting the most speed from the boat. The same thing applies to rudder markings, if you are allowed to race with an adjustable rudder. A rudder blade positioned straight down has less helm, less drag, and less control over the boat's heading. A rudder that is extended out at an angle creates more weather helm but also gives you more messages about what your boat wants to do.

Sailing to windward in light-to-moderate winds (2 to 12 knots), I like to see a centerboard angled back about 15 degrees. I believe any board that goes straight down is never going to be fast, and a 15-degree rake is a good starting place. As the wind increases and weather helm starts to appear, try pulling the board up some more. This moves your center of lateral resistance aft, and that should decrease your weather helm. If you are going to windward in very puffy conditions, you might try pulling the board up just a bit more to give the boat a chance to skid out to leeward and not be knocked over by a gust. If it is really puffy, with wind speeds of over 20 knots, you could do very well if you keep the angle of the board at something over 30 degrees.

Of course a lot of this depends on the size of your crew and how much leverage you can bring to bear to hold the rig down. The more leverage you have, the less need you have for the high-angled board. If you have a flexible rig, that itself is a kind of shock absorber for those heavy puffs. The leech of the mainsail opens up and the mainsail depowers. If you have enough crew weight in windy situations, you won't have to "reef" down the boat by pulling the centerboard up, dropping the travelers quickly, and changing tension on the outhaul, cunningham, and vang. If you don't have the leverage in a breeze, you can usually depower the main and still keep up your speed by using these centerboard and trimming techniques.

SAIL CARE

I'm often asked how long a sail is good for, and how one can tell when it is losing its power. Most racing sails that are not made of Mylar have a resinated finish to give them good shape retention. Some people say this makes for a short-lived sail, since if it starts to get soft it also starts to lose its power. While this is not always the case, there is little doubt that a sail with this type of finish can start to lose power after as few as fifteen to twenty races. But the Soling mainsail we used to win the Olympic Gold Medal at Kiel had over eighty races on it. Some sails can have as many as two hundred and fifty races on them without losing much power. There are exceptions to every rule, and a lot depends on where you sail and the care you give your sails.

Mylar sails are a significant development. Because the shape is built into a Mylar sail, it is difficult to alter its basic foil shape once it is set on the mast. Because these sails are harder to adjust, a good sailor who doesn't have a lot of time to practice with his Mylar sails might have a bit more trouble with them than he would with the more adjustable resinated sails.

I think you should have a new suit of sails every year if you are going to go after a major championship. And using a new sail requires breaking in that sail. Both the skipper and the crew must familiarize themselves with the new sail's shape and stiffness. When people ask me why the shape of their new sail is different from the old shape, I answer that the designed shape hasn't changed at all. It is just that the new sail is firmer and they'll have to adjust to it. A good way to deal with this transition is to use the new sail (after it is broken in) in the heavier conditions, and the old sail in light-to-moderate air. You will often get very good results by using the two sails in combination.

When you do get a new sail, you should put at least two races on it before you go into any championship series. To break in a new sail I like to go out in about 12 knots of wind, and I reach back and forth for an hour or more. Then I set my boat up for going to windward, and as I go on the wind, I start making my adjustments and watch the sail to see how it is reacting. One good variation on this routine is to reach back and forth for several hours, but once every hour to go on the wind and sail upward for fifteen minutes or so.

Never take a brand-new sail out in extremely heavy air and pull every control out to its maximum. You will give the sail a setback it may not recover from.

Wrinkles in sails are not always bad, and you should not panic if you have some. Many sails do have very firm wrinkles on either side of the tack. Those tack wrinkles should disappear when you apply some cunningham tension. Any wrinkles that appear around the tack area usually are there in direct proportion to the amount of additional roach that has been built into the luff of the sail.

There is no question that those who sail in fresh water have an advantage over those who don't, when it comes to sail maintenance. The reason is that freshwater sailors don't have to wash their sails off so much, and for this reason the sails tend to last a bit longer. But no matter where you sail, you should always fold your sails correctly. If you are sailing a small boat and are using either a firm-woven Dacron fabric or a sail constructed from Mylar film, you should roll up both your mainsail and jib. This keeps the surface of the sail smooth and it also keeps the sail at its maximum dimensions. If you crumple the sail up like a piece of paper, then try to smooth it out again, it will never be quite as large as it was before the crumpling took place.

If you are sailing in salt water, you should wash your sails off with fresh water at least once a week, and if you are in a major regatta it doesn't hurt to do it every day. This is an especially good idea whenever there is a light-air morning race followed by a heavy-air afternoon race—a racing situation that is very common in many parts of the world. The fresh water gets the salt spray off the sail material. Washing is especially helpful for spinnaker cloth, because the caked salt acts very much like a greasy film, and this can have a big effect on how the sail opens up during a hoist.

I never roll my spinnaker up into its launching profile until just before a race begins. For storage ashore I lay the sail out flat and fold it in half, putting the two clews together. Then I gently flake the material back and forth like a piece of yard goods. This keeps the fabric smooth, and because there are no creases, it remains at its maximum size.

Incidentally, if you are really interested in getting a good spinnaker hoist and set, sprinkle talcum powder on both sides of the sail just before you roll it up for the race. Talcum reduces friction and helps the sail open up without an hourglass in it. Even if you do happen to get a wrap in the sail, the talcum powder will let it unwind and get free more easily.

Every time you come in from sailing, check all the corners of your sails, because this is where they get the most wear. Also check the batten pockets, for they are another potential problem area. If you are going to be sailing in strong winds, don't hesitate to put a piece of duct tape over the outer end of the batten pocket to keep the batten from flying out. Take a piece of tape long enough to extend out a bit beyond the width of the batten pocket. Fold the tape over the leech of the sail so that half the tape is on one side and half on the other. This is a simple procedure that many good sailors are using and it will save you the embarrassment of having one of your battens fly out while you are maneuvering on the starting line in a heavy breeze with about thirty seconds left to the gun.

One very good way to damage your sails is to leave them inside a closed car with the sun beating down on them. Interior temperatures can easily reach 150 degrees, which will definitely affect the finish of the sail. The same rule applies when the time comes to put your sails away for the season. Always store them in a cool, dry place—and make sure they are dry when you store them, because even synthetics can mildew if there is moisture around.

This may sound funny, but I feel that sails can develop a personality—and you should know how you are going to react to this phenomenon, because there can be a wide variation in people's response. I have a friend in England who used to sail a Flying Dutchman with great success. He used the same mainsail for many years, well beyond what anyone in the class would normally think was its useful life. His reasoning was that he believed working on the finish of his hull was the most important thing he could do to prepare for his racing program. That, he thought, was how he could win races. Even though he sincerely thought it was his work on the hull that made him win, I never quite accepted that. I feel that because he knew he had an older sail, he steered his boat just a bit better than everyone else, and he paid more attention to his entire program of preparation. But even today he still is convinced that it was his sanding and polishing that gave him his winning edge.

Then there's the sailor who lives near me in Wisconsin. He is always letting people know he has a closetful of winners at home and he is continually trying to give those sails away. But for some reason no one wants them, even though I think he is closer to the truth than he thinks. It's my feeling that if he did pick out one of those sails, take it out, and work hard with it out on the water, eventually he would get a winning performance from it. But he doesn't really want to try. And that's why his closetful of "winners" gets bigger and bigger every year.

4

PREPARING
THE CREW

TEAMWORK

I suppose that secretly everybody wants to be a skipper. But there is also a great thrill in being part of a good crew. There is tremendous satisfaction when you make a good spinnaker set, or you sail by someone else in a hard-fought tacking duel. When you get into world-class competition, good crewwork is what makes the difference between two boats. Ninety percent of the difference lies in the boathandling: things like tacking, gybing, working the waves, and precision teamwork. At the top levels of racing everyone is going to have the best equipment, so your own boathandling skills and how you use your equipment are what is going to make the difference.

My great friend Andreas Josenhans is certainly one of the best crews in the world. (I should add, he is a successful skipper as well, but he genuinely enjoys being part of a crew.) He has the perfect physique for the boats I now spend much of my time racing (Andreas is 6 feet 1 inch tall and weighs around 220 pounds). But far more important is his will and desire to win. Andreas wants to win so badly that he will push himself harder than anyone else I have ever sailed with. He may be dead tired, but he won't quit hiking out, and he won't say a word about it. We have won two World Championships sailing together in the Star class, and many of the races were won because of Andreas's positive attitude and his incredible endurance in heavy-air conditions. Andreas also enjoys working hard on all the things that have to be done ashore before a race to get the boat, and ourselves, ready: things like the sanding, the rubbing, and the polishing. On the water he knows all there is to know about sail shape, the compass, course position, boathandling, and the opposition's whereabouts. When we are sailing together I know exactly where the other boats are without having to turn my head, because Andreas is constantly feeding me the information.

Some crews can give me compass headings and tell me which boat is doing what. But after a while I ask them if they could please be just a bit more quiet. They're giving me lots of information, but they're not interpreting it, and therefore it's almost useless. Andreas has the rare ability to take the information he has, apply that to what he already knows, analyze it, and then give me just the right amount of necessary raw data along with his own interpretation and suggestions for what might be done. This is the kind of thinking—thoughtfulness, really—that can greatly help a skipper. Andreas gives me, in one crisp sentence, where the other boats are, how their jib and main travelers are set, how much backstay they have, and what kind of rake the masts have. And I get all this delivered in a level, calm tone of voice.

Some crews don't like to say anything at all when they get behind. But that is when Andreas proves even more valuable; whenever we are behind, we always seem to be able to analyze our information and work our way up through the fleet. I can't think of any race we have sailed together in which we have gone backward in our standings during that race, with the possible exception of a change of position caused by an unexpected windshift. And even after the wind has shifted, we usually pick ourselves up again and start moving back up through the fleet.

Many crews like to relax during downwind sailing, especially when it involves keeping track of the compass. Andreas works even harder on the runs, and I can think of several times when we've been able to stay on the inside of a shift because he is watching the compass and is also thinking about what is going on around us.

At the start of a race Andreas calls out the time, but in addition, his position and attitude just before the start often keep another boat from trying to squeeze in underneath us. He will sit there on the windward rail and stare hard at a boat headed toward us down to leeward, and that crew will take a look at him and then decide to head off and go somewhere else. They don't want to tangle with Andreas! Then, right at the gun, there he is, hiked out hard over the side of the boat and putting his maximum effort and power into holding the boat down. The result is that we go tearing out of the starting blocks and get away from the boats around us with clear air.

Andreas's burning enthusiasm, his desire to win, and his effervescence are so contagious that they make me want to do my very best. In fact, when we are racing together, I feel badly if, when I happen to look around, I lose my concentration and drop back a yard or two. I don't feel I have lost distance against the fleet; rather I feel I have lost some of the distance that Andreas has worked so hard to get. It is *his* yardage that I have lost.

And this leads me to make a few more observations about what sort of crew you might like to have on board. I always try to get a crew whose personality traits are different from my own and those of all the other people on board. I think this difference makes it easier, especially if you are planning a long campaign. If you have a crew of three people, for example, two of them might start working on the other one if they are too much alike. Opposites, I think, do have a tendency to be more compatible. If you have two people whose personalities are similar, try hard to find a third individual who can provide a balance and counterforce to the other two.

In fact, if I am involved in a very long campaign that will go over an entire summer or longer, I am convinced that next to the desire to win and personal optimism, the most important requirement for any crew is compatibility. Sailing knowledge and good physical conditioning come next. But everything else, particularly the onboard maneuvers, can be taught and learned as long as there is the genuine desire to set a certain goal and work hard for it.

I've seen a number of very good crews get into trouble because they can't get along with each other, and almost always the result is a poor performance on the racecourse. Very often the crews are excellent sailors individually, but the chemistry between them just isn't right. Teamwork is a critical part of sailboat racing, so it is worth spending time to get crews who can complement your own personality.

I don't think it is necessary for a crew to spend a lot of time together socially. My crew is often at least twenty years younger than I am, so I have to work hard to bridge the generation gap. This does require an extra effort, and perhaps that is why some older skippers prefer to sail with older crews. I think that also is why many of these older skippers don't sail as fast as they could. In sailboat racing you have to keep youth up in front of you—in the crew spots where you need to have quickness. If you don't have that speed in the hands and the body, you are sure to be beaten.

I work hard in training to get to the point where everyone can anticipate every possible maneuver before it happens. You, as skipper, shouldn't have to say anything. If, for example, you decide to tack, all it should take to get people moving is the different motion of the boat as it starts to come up into the wind. If you're sailing a one-design boat, the crew should automatically come up on the rail and hike out hard to pull the boat over on top of them in a classic roll-tacking maneuver. Then they should go across together to the other side in one smooth movement.

SPECIAL SITUATIONS

I like to prepare a number of variations on the standard maneuvers. I suppose you could describe them as "special"

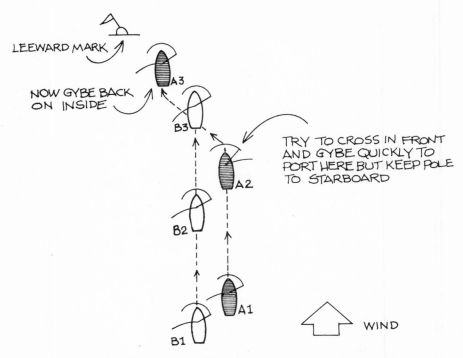

LEEWARD MARK

NOW GYBE BACK ON INSIDE

TRY TO CROSS IN FRONT AND GYBE QUICKLY TO PORT HERE BUT KEEP POLE TO STARBOARD

A3

B3

A2

B2

A1

B1

WIND

Fig. 4-1. A nonstandard procedure like this "Gluek" can be practiced ahead of time so that in a race only one word need be used to call for the maneuver.

maneuvers that apply to certain tactical situations that I know could occur in a race. I work on these special drills in practice sessions, because if I had to explain, during a race, what maneuver I think is going to work, and then describe how to do it, I'd wind up making a very long speech! And the time for action would have come and gone before anything was done. No one has time to listen in a race. So what I do is to set up the maneuver in practice, give it a name, and then, when the time seems right out on the racecourse, I just say the name and everyone immediately knows what is coming next.

For example, I might say "let's give them a Gluek," and everyone on board will know what to do. Now, John Gluek happens to be a very fine sailor, and because we have sailed together in many campaigns we have cooked up a maneuver that bears his name. After we have practiced it, I can use just that one name to call for this interesting tactic.

You might do a Gluek when you are running downwind on the starboard tack and you have moved just in front of another boat that is to leeward of you. You'd like to gybe and see if you can get across in front of it and get the leeward position. The key to this maneuver is that nobody on board moves a muscle. You quickly gybe the mainsail over to port and, at the same time, have one of the crew hold the new spinnaker guy out as far as possible and keep the spinnaker full even though the pole is still on the starboard tack (Fig. 4-1). If you see that you are *not* going to be able to get across the bow of the other boat, you can quickly gybe the mainsail back onto the starboard and proceed. Sometimes, when you gybe your mainsail back to starboard, the other boat's spinnaker will collapse for a split second as the air spills off the end of your main. The Gluek can be a terrific offensive move.

But my main point here is that you can develop a very precisely customized maneuver ahead of time. Put a name on it, and when the time comes, you can move quickly and everyone will know just what to do.

TRAVEL

I like to have all the crew travel together to a regatta so everyone gets involved in working up to what I call complete mental readiness. But somehow, in this day and age, we seem less able to do this and what happens more often is that some crewmembers fly in and others sail or drive the boat and equipment.

What that really means is that you have to get all your inventory lists organized well ahead of the time the boat is set to leave. I keep complete lists of gear to take: tools, sails, spare parts, and clothing. And I like to have one person in charge of each list. This gets everyone involved in the mental countdown before the racing starts.

FOOD

It's important to pay careful attention to your diet when you are away from home. I've sailed with crews that have a single gulp of orange juice and half a piece of toast for breakfast, either because they are on a diet or they are in a rush. I have a lot of trouble with that approach, because I think an early but nourishing breakfast is a very important part of the daily routine, particularly when a morning race is scheduled. About an hour before the start of a race, I like to pass out a candy bar to get everyone revved up.

Drinking lots of water is something many crews overlook. Make sure you always carry enough water aboard to avoid dehydration problems. You have to be particularly careful in warmer climates, where evaporation occurs much more quickly than you think, and it seems that sailing on salt water exacerbates the problem. The main symptom of dehydration is headache, and if you have a bad one it can certainly affect your ability to think clearly. In most cases all it takes to cure the problem is a swallow or two of water, so it is just plain foolish not to have a container on board.

If two races are scheduled for one day, or even if there is only one afternoon race, I skip lunch—except for the candy bar I've already mentioned. My reason is that the way I sit or hike on a boat, particularly a small one, is not at all helpful to my digestive process. I've found that whenever I eat something too soon before the start of a race, I develop some pretty bad stomach cramps soon after I start hiking out. I'm sure that other sailors can handle this without problems, but I have made it a practice to skip lunch if I'm at all unsure about whether there is going to be enough time to get it well digested before race time.

One final thought about the crew: never forget that when you win a race, everyone on the boat wins the race. You have got to share the victory, for you are never going to be any better than your crew. There are plenty of skippers who forget this, and perhaps that is part of the reason why they don't finish as well as they should.

There is no question that preparation of the equipment plays a big role in sailing, but the human side is an equally important part of the sport; if you are really serious about doing well in competition, you must spend a lot of time selecting a crew that can work well together. And working well together means not only having all the necessary sailing skills, but also having the less tangible qualities of enthusiasm and compatibility. Very often these two ingredients are the ones that provide the winning margin. Almost every one of the successful sailors I know understands this, and they work very hard to get just the right combination of personalities on board. They know that when everything else is equal, it is the spirit of the crew that is going to make the difference when they are approaching the finish line.

5

UNDERSTANDING THE ELEMENTS

WIND

I have always been a student of the weather, and I have studied the weather enough to know that however much you learn and whatever you do, it still can get you into deep trouble on the racecourse. Even so, you do have to know as much as you can about the wind, clouds, rain, fog, and water temperature. All of these can have a big effect on the outcome of a race. And they can be helpful during a race: if you find yourself on the wrong side of a 30-degree windshift, the chances are that the clouds could have told you what was going to happen; every time you see a black squall, you should know to sail toward it, for that's where the wind is.

I don't want to say anything unkind about the science of meteorology, for there is certainly a place for it in the world of sailboat racing. But it is too much to expect a meteorologist to guess what a very local wind condition and wind direction will be for a particular day.

You should always get a daily weather forecast, though, for it is very helpful in giving you predicted wind strengths, and that can affect your sail selection. On a race day, get your weather forecast, but wait as long as you can before you make your final sail selection. Always take the sails that will be the most effective for the wind velocity that exists on the first windward leg: It always is much easier later in a race to defend from a leading position than it is to attack against someone who is already ahead of you.

If I hear a forecast predicting winds of up to 20 knots late in the day, but only 10 knots at the start, I would save my heavy-weather sails, because were I to use them I'd be so sluggish on the first beat that I'd never catch up, even though I might have blazing speed on that final heavy-weather beat to the finish. On a conventional Olympic course you have to sail to windward three times. In this case I have the correct sails on the first windward leg, those same sails will be almost right on the second beat, and I can always defend myself on the third once I get ahead.

The important thing to do on the course is to develop an ability to look ahead and see what the velocity of the wind is going to be and then set your boat up for that expected wind speed. This means being able to read the wind velocity as you see it out on the water, for knowing what the wind speed is going to be affects how you are going to sail to windward. Many boats can sail a considerably higher close-hauled course once they get just a bit more wind velocity. With some keelboats, sailing in light-to-moderate conditions, an increase of 5 knots of wind speed can mean sailing 5 degrees, or more, above the previous course. That's a lot.

An equally important skill to develop is being able to see the wind, then anticipating when it will reach you so you don't waste a second. If you can concentrate on a wall of wind coming at you and sail up to it just as your competition tacks and sails away toward what you know is a lower velocity, that guarantees that you will pick up ground.

To calculate what the wind velocity is going to be, look at the waves and ripples on the surface. The color and texture of water changes: it becomes darker as the higher winds move across the surface. Sunglasses heighten this contrast and can help make the wind easier to read. You can also pick up some early clues by looking at other boats, flags, or other landmarks that are visible on the horizon.

Predicting Shifts

You must also know whether the wind is blowing in cycles. It often does this, first *veering* (or going to the right), then *backing* (going to the left). This is where a good crew and good compass work can really help. If you have time before the start (and you should try to make the time), sail upwind along the track to the windward mark and write down your headings for both the port and starboard tacks on the deck. Take and record several readings on both tacks at five-minute intervals and see if there is any trend.

On a race day, right after I leave the harbor area on my way to the start, I begin by going head-to-wind, and I write that figure down. Then I sail along for ten or fifteen more minutes and I go head-to-wind again and write that heading down. I will have done this several more times before I get to the starting area and begin my practice run up the course. Now I have enough wind-direction readings to tell me the probable shifting sequence of the wind. You would be surprised how often this windshift message is out there, as plain as the nose on your face, and how often it is missed because people just don't bother to do their homework.

One fairly reliable rule is that every time the wind backs in the northern hemisphere, it always veers once more before it backs again. And if it is continuing to back, it will also continue shifting in this pattern. And very often if the wind builds up in strength during the day, it is also going to veer as the day goes on. Tactically, this means that you should favor the right side of the course over the left as you beat to windward—though I am afraid there are just enough exceptions to this so that you should probably judge each case separately.

Once I was sailing a 5.5-Meter in Norway with Albert Fay. We took our wind readings faithfully for over an hour as we went out to the starting line. Our readings showed us that the wind was definitely veering, and we concluded that we should head for the right side of the course as soon as we could after the start. However, the starting line was heavily favored at the port end. We decided to make a port-tack approach at the favored end, but we were a bit too early getting to the line. We went over the line, gybed around to the outside of the mark in a nice power loop, and came back again on port, sailing toward the fleet that now was starting on starboard tack in front of us. We saw a hole in the line of boats, shot through it on port, and started moving away from the rest of the boats out to the right side. Sure enough, we started getting headed bit by bit as the wind began shifting to the right.

But we also knew from our thorough prerace measurements that the wind was going to shift back again. So we tacked and sailed across the fleet on a very high starboard tack until we got the predicted header. Then we tacked over onto port to catch the next phasing shift. Finally we tacked again, 600 yards in front of the second-place boat.

The point of this story is that we had figured all this out well before the start. There wasn't any real magic, and you could see what was happening if you were looking for it on the water. Once we knew what the rhythm of the wind was, we stuck with it and we were successful.

The Persistent Shift

A persistent shift is basically one that just keeps going in one direction without any of the usual backing and filling. It's an extraordinary phenomenon, the type of shift that you really have to watch out for.

I learned a good lesson about what a persistent shift can do to you in a Soling World Championship in Sweden. We were using a gate start, also known as a rabbit start. I didn't do a very good job getting away from the line on starboard tack, and soon someone sailed over the top of us. We had to tack to port to get away, and when we did, we had to go astern of nearly every one of the sixty-six boats out there.

When we finally got to the windward end of that fleet and tacked back onto starboard, we didn't look too bad. In fact we

could see the entire fleet through our window on the mainsail. But then the compass started to give us the bad news. It
started to say the wind was backing quickly. We were being
headed badly, so we tacked back onto port, thinking this was
a good idea. Then we looked over at the boats that had
continued on out starboard. They now had tacked over onto
port and were half a mile directly to windward. They had
sailed one tack almost half the distance of the windward leg,
even though they were taking a terrible beating on the starboard tack as they went out. We rounded the weather mark
in sixty-sixth place, five minutes behind the leading boat.

What we didn't know was that we were in a persistent shift
that was constantly backing. We did not spot it because the
shift only took place once our boat was clear of the starting
area and this was one race where we hadn't bothered to sail
up the first weather leg to see what was going on. If we had
done so, we would have been a lot smarter than we were. The
second time we sailed up that leg we knew better and we
spent almost the entire windward leg on the starboard tack
and sailed only about two minutes on the port. I tried reading
this persistent shift in the clouds and on the water but I just
couldn't see anything. It was there, though, and it was probably the worst one I have ever been in.

Gusts and Clouds

Though the wind direction on a racecourse can have a high
degree of predictability if you have done your homework,
there are some other points to keep in mind.

First, you must know how to handle a gust that is coming at
you. Look at the band of wind as it approaches and try to
figure out which tack you should be on to take maximum
advantage of the puff. If you are on starboard tack and you
see that the wind is coming directly toward you without any
change in direction, the puff probably is going to be a header,
and you should get set to go onto port tack just as it arrives.

If you see some horizontal movement in the wind band that
shows the gust is moving from your right to your left (if you
are on starboard tack), plan on getting a lift; you should stay on

the same tack and start to head up as it hits. If you see more wind well up to windward, either tack to get over to it or start pinching up slightly so you can get up to it without tacking. Pinching up to get in a better breeze is an especially good technique to use when you are lake sailing. But the important thing is to go right after the wind, wherever it is. You have got to get the jump on your competitors.

If I am sailing on a lake, I like to tack just as the new wind hits me. On larger bodies of water—big lakes and the ocean—you don't get the very sharp changes in direction, so I like to hold on for several boat lengths to make sure I'm in a new wind and its direction is stable.

Stability, incidentally, is another important element in all windshifts. When you are sailing in a changing season, early spring or early fall, the water temperature is going to be quite different from the air temperature. The new effect is that you are involved with air that is subjected to a tumbling action and this changes the normal horizontal flow of wind over the water, either increasing or decreasing its speed by a dramatic amount.

For example, water colder than 50 degrees can often kill a warming land breeze in the spring of the year. At the very least, its direction and speed are going to be very unpredictable. In the fall you have exactly the reverse situation. With colder air coming over warmer water you often get increased wind speeds but equally unpredictable directions. If you sail in either of these conditions, you have to keep your eyes open and use all the visual clues you can to find out what is going on. You might even have to sail the windward legs a little less conservatively, and you should be prepared to sail a bit farther out to one side of the course on the windward and leeward legs. Any race or series that is sailed under such conditions is bound to be interesting, but also a bit frustrating.

A word about clouds: they help you. Always sail toward clouds and try to get under them, for that is where the best wind is going to be. This is especially true in cases where there seems to be considerable moisture in the clouds and a lot of open water relative to the land masses around.

Land Effects

A land mass can have an effect on the wind blowing on a racecourse from a distance as great as three miles. This means local knowledge about an area is important; you should always study the local geography and get a feel for how a point of land might affect things. Never be both the judge and the jury in any of this, though; when you are in doubt, always follow the flow of boats. Go with the fleet and then use your own personal evaluation to favor one side of the course by perhaps four to five boat lengths.

When wind flows on or off a shore it usually arrives and leaves the land at about a 90-degree angle. This means that if you are beating to windward, the windward shore is always the place to be, for this is where you are going to get your lifts. In lake sailing it is true that you get a steadier wind in the center of the lake. But by the time the wind gets out there it has gone through a fanning effect, and that greatly modifies

Fig. 5-1. When approaching a point of land, sail toward the point until you hit a header caused by the flow coming off the point. Then tack offshore until you pick up another header from the more normal flow away from the land. Then tack back in to the shore again.

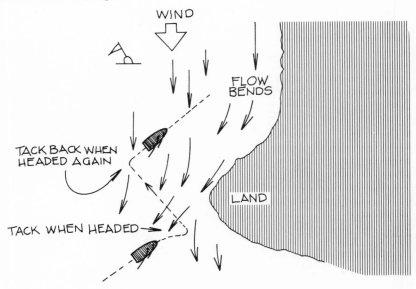

and generally reduces the initial speed of the wind as it comes off the land and attaches to the water.

If there is a point of land ahead of you, always sail up to the point but no further. Then you should tack and go offshore. If you go beyond that point of land on the same tack, you are going to sail into a bad header that is created by the wind as it bends along the windward shore. Once you tack offshore, sail out until you get the next big shift that is leaving the shore. Then tack and go back in again toward the shore (Fig. 5-1).

If you are beating to windward on the starboard tack and some boats underneath and ahead of you get headed 30 degrees, don't panic. Keep sailing straight ahead and don't tack. Stay with those boats until you also get into the new air. Then you can tack onto port and come back with the flow of the fleet. Now if the wind starts to head you on the port tack, and you pick it up on your compass right away, try tacking back onto your original starboard tack. You might pick up some boats, because now you should be able to stay in this new shaft of air longer than the boats above you. You should also be able to get to the next new shaft first because now you are ahead of the other boats in terms of distance sailed up the course.

Anticipating Shifts

What is the best way to tell when you are going to get a windshift? My experience is that if there is going to be a significant shift, the wind speed drops slightly just before the shift comes. If, for example, you are sailing along on a high port tack and you go into a lull, start looking down to leeward, because the chances are excellent that new air is coming in and stopping this flow. The two flows are merging and you are in no-man's-land. So sail on until you reach the new breeze. If you are on a high starboard tack and the wind drops, do the same thing. Look for a shift, because two winds are working against each other.

Always look at your compass to get your final confirmation. The reason is that boats racing today, especially the high-performance keelboats, are very close-winded, and they are sensitive not only to wind direction but to wind strength. If your crew tells you that you are now down 5 degrees on the compass heading, you, as skipper, must know what the wind velocity is and whether it is up or down. In this case, if you know the wind has also gone down 5 knots, you should keep on going. But if you are down 5 degrees on the compass and the wind velocity has increased, you are in a header and you ought to tack immediately.

If there is a hole on the course—a place where there is no wind—and you sail into it, you have only yourself to blame, for you must have been staring at your bowplate. You haven't projected yourself up (or down) the course and you haven't bothered to look around. Projecting yourself up the course is a lot like keeping yourself from falling off a cliff. You always have to keep your eyes open. If you are lucky enough to be leading and everyone around you wants to sail into a hole, you really don't have any choice except to sail in there with them and hope that because you are in the lead, you will get out to the new air first—and that's probably what will happen.

CURRENTS

As for current, there are those who say that two boats racing on the same course are affected by current equally, no matter what tack they are on. I'm not sure about this, for it is my feeling that any bottom contour, whether sea or lake, has a big effect on surface water flow, and it is not a constant across any distance. Because there are these rivers of current in most places you will sail, they are going to act on the boat differently depending where you are on the course.

Lee-Bow Effect

This brings up the famous lee-bow effect. If the current is coming at you at an angle that is very close to the course you are sailing and if, by pinching just a bit, you can get your lee bow into the flow of the current, the movement of the water is going to push against the hull, the keel, and the rudder, and it is going to drive you up to windward even though you are going slower over the bottom. If you are on the other tack, the current is going to be hitting you broadside and pushing you down. If you can get the lee-bow effect to push you to windward, I feel you also increase the wind pressure on the sails. If I am on the tack that goes across the current I feel I am losing speed and distance to the mark. That is why, unless there is an obvious way to get out of the current entirely, or at least to a slower flow, I think you should always make your longest tack to the next mark sailing in the lee-bow position. And I would do this even if it means pinching a bit to do so.

If there is any chance of the wind dropping as you sail upwind, my feeling is that you should always begin by sailing into the current, and at the best angle you can make. You want to make the maximum amount of headway toward the next mark while the wind has the power to get you upstream.

Calculating Current

Check to see which way the current is setting on the course before a race by carrying a tide stick on the boat. Take a wooden batten and tape a shackle to it at one end so that the top of the stick floats about an inch above the water surface. You can get fancier and take a plastic tube, plug one end, put a little lead into the other, and seal it with epoxy. Make the stick 3 feet long for best results, and design it so that only 1 inch is sticking out of the water (so it isn't affected by waves). Put the stick in the water at whatever mark you are interested in, then time it to see how far it drifts. You can make up a little chart and put it on the deck: for example, 100 feet of drift in one minute equals 1 knot, etc. Using the tide stick and the mark as a range, line the bow of your boat up on that range to get a reciprocal of the flow's compass direction.

If you have time, take current readings on both sides of the course. You can do this by using a balloon, some line, and a lead fish sinker. Anchor the balloon, then proceed with your calculations as though it were a mark.

What you get from knowing the speed and direction of the current is an understanding of the nature of the flow and whether you are approaching a lee bow as you go to wind-

ward on one tack or the other. Every time I have taken the
time to get current readings, it has made a big difference in
my sailing efficiency.

Current Tactics

If you feel the wind is going to be decreasing during a beat,
you should sail up beyond the mark, then tack over and sail
toward it across the current. If you are at the beginning of a
reach and the current is crossing from right to left across the
course, you should immediately sail high of the actual compass course. This gets you sailing closer to the wind, which
increases the apparent wind and therefore your boatspeed.
Later, the current should set you back down to the course line
again near the mark. To hold your position relative to the
mark, line the mark up with an object ashore or a point on the
horizon, and don't let the mark move to either side of the
object. This is called using the *gunsight* method. If the wind
does come up on the reach, you can head off and build up a
little more speed. Head up a little if the wind drops.

If there is a current moving from right to left on a reaching
leg, I might stay above the actual compass course to the mark
for as much as one-third of the leg, then use the gunsight
approach to bring me in on the mark. There is no hard-and-
fast mathematical solution to any of this, though, and you
always have to let your competition tell you how to handle
your sailing angles. If you get too technical, you'll wind up
outsmarting yourself as you sail away from the boats you are
trying to beat!

If you go around a gybe mark on an Olympic course and the
tide is pushing you from right to left, consider sailing off well
to leeward of the new course to the leeward mark if you can
do so without running into disturbed air from other boats.
When I go around the gybe mark, I always look at it to see
whether the current is flowing in the same direction as it was
at the windward mark. If it is, and the flow is from right to
left, my first thought always is to try breaking away low.
Often you can pick up a considerable amount of ground, and
it is a good maneuver if you think the wind is going to drop on

your way down the leg. Once you are below the straight-line compass course to the mark, you can head up as you approach it and increase your apparent wind—and that will improve your boatspeed over all the boats that have stayed inside you to windward. They, on the other hand, will be set up above the mark and they will have to head off to maintain their position on the line to the mark. This means they are going to be sailing in reduced apparent wind speeds.

Current is often a big factor in a race; you can't ever afford to overlook its effects. If you know what it is going to do before you get on the course, you are way ahead of those skippers who know nothing. However, you should never let yourself get too far away from any of the boats around you just because you have become enthralled with some mathematical solution involving current. Even though you may be correct, you shouldn't expose yourself too much to the theoretical. Instead, stay close to your competition. Stay with the flow of the fleet and cover them if you have to.

When it comes to current, it doesn't pay to go out on a limb and sail off by yourself. On a short closed course, the chances are too great that someone will saw that limb off, and you will be left hanging as the rest of the fleet sails off in front of you.

6

ON THE COURSE

BEFORE THE RACE

To make sure you get off on the right foot, always sail your best on the way out to the starting line. You may think this is unimportant, but it can have a big effect on how your competitors "see" you. The way you sit in the boat and the way you talk to other boats around you makes an impression. Sure, there may be three or four boats—maybe as many as ten if it is a World Championship—that won't care one way or the other. But if you handle your boat with confidence, the impression you leave with others might help you work yourself in on a starting line or at some other place along the course.

Plan things so you are in the starting area at least thirty minutes before the first gun. But as soon as you have cleared the harbor, start taking true wind headings and writing them down. Have at least eight of them by the time you reach the starting area. Now try to sail, at the minimum, half the distance of the first windward leg. As you beat to windward, try to learn the rhythm of the waves. Also check the compass heading every five minutes. Go head-to-wind and record that as well as the close-hauled headings for both tacks. Write these numbers down on the deck, port and starboard, using a lead pencil. If you sail a dinghy or a trapeze boat, you might build a clear-film patch pocket into your windsuit and use a grease pencil on the film. This is an excellent way for a trapeze crew to keep track of compass headings as the race progresses.

The headings you get as you sail up the course the first time are going to be different from the ones you get the second time up. And that is why it is important to have a written record. If the headings on the second beat are higher (or lower) than they were the first time up the course, the crew should let the skipper know about it immediately.

Reading the Line

If you are racing in a large fleet, the way the starting line is set relative to the direction of the wind and to the course to the first windward mark becomes critical. You must determine exactly how the line is set; the only accurate way to know this is to use a compass. You begin by sailing onto the starting line at the committee-boat end on starboard tack. When you feel you are up on the line, turn down along the line and sight the mast and forestay toward the mark located at the other end. Simultaneously get the crew forward to look astern and line up the rudder post and the backstay, or the middle of the transom, with the flag on the committee boat. A racing stripe running down the center of the boat can be very helpful here, and some racing sailors have a stripe running down the middle of the boat for just this purpose.

When your boat is on the line and lined up fore-and-aft with the two marks at either end, get the compass heading and write it down. This figure gives you the set of the line, in degrees. Now add 90 degrees to that to get the square-to-the-line. Then go head-to-wind and get the true wind heading. If the true wind is the same as your square-to-the-line figure, there is no favor and you can, theoretically anyway, start at either end of the line or anywhere in the middle.

For example, if you run the line on starboard tack and you

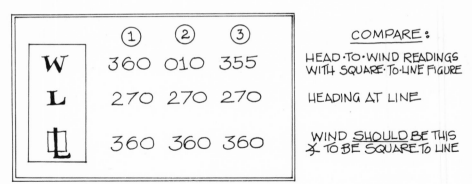

Fig. 6-1. To determine whether there is a favor on the starting line, the first thing to do is to write down W (wind) L (line) and the figure that is (mathematically) square to the line. Then run the line and record its direction. In this example the line (L) is 270°, which means that square to the line is 360°. Now go head to wind and compare it with the square-to-the-line figure. In case #1, wind is 360° and there is no favor. But in both case #2 and case #3 there is a difference between wind and square-to-the-line. In case #2 there is a 10° favor for the starboard tack; in case #3 there is a 5° favor for the port tack.

get a compass heading of 270 degrees, this means that the square-to-the-line figure is 360 degrees (270 plus 90). But if you go head-to-wind and find that the true wind is 010 degrees, you know the line is not set square to the wind, and the committee-boat end is favored by 10 degrees (Fig. 6-1).

Keep two things in mind when you go head-to-wind to take your readings. First, decide what telltales you are going to use. On a boat with a nonoverlapping jib, I like to use my entire jib, and I try to get as much of it on centerline as I can. Second, make sure you come to a complete stop and you let your compass settle down after making a sharp turn to windward. I stop and I might even let the boat back up a little. I also get *three* marks each time I go head-to-wind, because something might not be right with one of them. Then I average the three to get the true wind direction. Never take a wind reading if there is a boat crossing in front, because you will always get a distorted reading. Stay in clear air even if it means sailing out in front of the line a short distance, or going outside one end of the starting line.

Always keep your eye on the starting line, and make sure

the crew aboard the committee boat doesn't change the amount of anchor line they have let out. If nothing has been touched on the committee boat, you can go head-to-wind up to thirty seconds before the actual start and pick up a new windshift.

If you don't have a compass, you have to use a seat-of-the-pants system; there are only two good ones. The first is to come head-to-wind and look at the bow of your boat. Whichever end of the line it is pointing to is the favored end. The second method is to sail along the line on starboard tack and trim your sails so they are just on the verge of luffing. Then, without changing the trim of the sails, turn around and sail back toward the committee boat. If the sails now are very full you know that the pin end of the line is the favored one, for the wind obviously is blowing more from the left side of the course.

If you use the head-to-wind method, always try to run head-to-wind both at the committee boat end and at the pin end. Then compare the two. Often you get different readings. During the ten-minute sequence you should take several readings at the pin end, and you might even take one fifty yards outside the line. Then do the same thing fifty yards beyond the committee-boat end. You will be surprised how often there is a substantial difference in wind direction from one end of the line to the other.

This is the kind of information you can plug into your overall race strategy. For example, you might have a heavy port-tack favor at the pin but you know from your other observations that the wind will probably swing to the right soon after the start. This means that if you decide to go for a pin-end start to catch the port-tack favor on the line, you'd better be there right on time, and plan to break through and go out to the right side of the course immediately. As a practical matter, if you think the wind is going to go to the right after the start, you are going to have real trouble getting yourself clear of the left side of the fleet anyway. This is one case where I would give up the port-tack favor at the pin end and I would plan to start either in the middle of the line or

perhaps even at the upper or committee-boat end of the line.
The reason is that I want to be free to tack my boat quickly
and get over to the right side of the course. If a starting line is
square-to-the-wind, I prefer to start somewhere along the
upper half of the line.

Before the five-minute gun goes off you should know which
end of the line you want to head for, though you must remain
flexible as long as you can in case there is a sudden windshift.
In certain conditions, especially those you are apt to find on a
lake, try to keep all your options open up to two minutes
before the starting gun, though this depends on how long it
takes you to sail from one end of the line to the other. In a
high-performance dinghy you should be able to sail the full
length of the line in about one and a half minutes. With a
keelboat and a large fleet, it could take you up to three
minutes to complete the run. (It's a good idea to time how
long it takes you to sail the length of the line while you are
getting your compass course to determine the set of the line.)
When you know how long it takes you to sail from one end of
the line to the other, you'll be able to make quick adjustments
during your approach. If the wind shifts when you are in your
final starting sequence, you can check your position relative
to either end of the line, look at how much time you have left,
and make an intelligent decision about whether there is
enough time to get to the favored end before the start.

Unless you are a singlehander, always have someone else
call out the time before the start. If you have to look down at
your own watch constantly, someone is bound to come up to
leeward of you and pull the wool over your eyes. As skipper
you must concentrate completely on three things: the boats
around you, the sheeting of your sails, and your position on
the line. In the warning period (ten to five minutes before the
start) I like to hear the time left to the next gun called out
every minute up to thirty seconds to the gun. At that point, I
like to hear the remaining time at fifteen seconds, then ten
seconds, and finally a countdown to the gun.

In the preparatory sequence (five minutes to the start) I like
the time called out every thirty seconds down to the two-

minute mark. Then I might check the wind one more time by coming head-to-wind as the counting sequence continues, in fifteen-second intervals, down to one minute. From this point on I like the time called every five seconds down to the twenty-second mark and then every second until the gun.

Make sure that whoever does call out the time does it in a calm voice, and not one that is so loud every boat in the fleet can hear it. Very often I hear boats next to me counting down the last thirty seconds; I also hear their discussions on tactics. Obviously I'm ready for them when they do move. If you stay quiet you won't give away what you are going to do before you actually do it.

If you have three or more people on board, a crew in the middle of the boat should call the time. The person farthest forward should watch the starting line and make sure the boat is right up there on the line when the gun goes. That person should also be in charge of calling out the boats just to leeward and to windward, though everyone should be alert to a boat swinging up underneath you at the last moment. One good way to tell when you are up on the line is to run the line well before the start. Pick an object ashore and line it up with the starting mark, then use the two objects as a range. When the two are lined up on your final approach, you know you are up on the line.

If the compass course to the windward mark is posted on the side of the committee boat, write it down, along with the courses for the other legs. By the time the gun goes you should have recorded the set of the line, true wind heading, the amount one end is favored, the port and starboard tack headings, the compass courses to all the various racing marks, and any wind oscillations you have noticed on your practice run up the first weather leg. Make sure all the numbers are located in a place where the crew can see them on both tacks, even when they are hiked out.

Carving a Hole

Carving a hole in the line is a technique you have to know how to perform if you want to get a good start in a fleet of any size. Carving requires good teamwork and excellent boat-handling skills, for you must constantly start and stop your boat and head it into, or turn it away from, the wind. And this good teamwork will intimidate the skippers around you. If you can maneuver crisply and the other boats know you are very alert to what is going on, they are far more likely to sail off down the line and try to get into line somewhere else.

What you are doing when you carve a hole is forcing the boat(s) above you to head up into the wind; as you go with them, you begin to open up some space below you where there are no boats. You start this carving process by attaching an overlap on the boat immediately to windward. Then slowly head up and squeeze that boat to windward. You can sail at least a close-haul course before the gun, and you can squeeze the boat up enough so you can create a hole, or open space of water, to leeward of you. You can use that open water to head off at just the proper time and get yourself moving at top speed before the boats to windward of you. The bigger the hole is to leeward, the sooner you can fall off and start building up your speed. When the time does come to head off, trim the sails to their optimum shape and, if there is a breeze, get out on the rail and hike hard (Fig. 6-2).

Fig. 6-2. To carve a hole among a group of boats on the starting line, first establish an overlap on the boat to windward. Then slowly head up to create an open space to leeward. At the proper time, just before the start, head off into the open space, sheet in the sails, and build up to maximum speed.

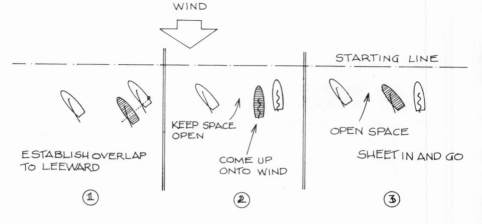

If all these adjustments and movements aren't done correctly, your boat is just going to heel over on its side and it won't accelerate. If you are in a keelboat you can head off ten seconds before the starting gun and you will be going close to full speed and be right on the target. In a dinghy or high-performance centerboarder, five seconds should give you time to hit the line going at full speed.

Position on the Line

In any timed start, exactly where you want to be on the line really depends on how much one end of the line is favored, or what you think the wind is going to do soon after the start. These factors are what determine where you head and which side of the course you want to protect on the way up to the weather mark. If, for example, you think the wind is going to shift to the right after the start, you want to be on the right side of the fleet (the committee-boat end). But if you think the wind is going to swing to the left after the start, then you want to be much farther down the line toward the pin.

If you don't anticipate a major shift either way, it's a good idea to go off the line on starboard one-third of the way down from the committee boat if for no other reason than the area is less likely to have a lot of congestion. This is especially true if the line is slightly favored to starboard. The best sailors usually can muster the necessary speed to accelerate away quickly from the mass of boats right after the starting gun has fired, and this is why you usually see them start either one-third of the way down from the committee-boat end or one-third of the way up from the pin end.

I'm kind of an exception to this rule, because for many years I preferred to start down at the pin end. I was very happy there, and if the line had a good port-end favor we had enough acceleration and speed so that we could go off on starboard tack at the pin end, tack onto port several minutes later and have the entire fleet underneath us. But if you are unsure about your boatspeed compared to the others, the best thing to do is to think hard about what the wind might do, then try to get either the pin or the committee-boat end of the line and hope you can hold on in the footrace to the windward mark.

If one end of the line is favored by more than 10 degrees, that side of the course clearly needs to be protected. Even if there is only a 7-degree favor I would try hard to win the committee-boat end of the line. In fact, I would work much harder at it than I would if the port end were favored by 7 degrees. The reason is that if you are successful, you will have the entire fleet to leeward of you and will be in the control position.

THE START

Starboard-Tack Start

When using a starboard-tack approach, *never* run parallel to the line on starboard tack two to three boat lengths back of the line and look for an open space you can sail into. That always invites trouble: first, because of the speed you can build up as you sail behind the line; and second, because of the maneuvering you have to do to keep clear of other boats as you try to get into a clear space.

I always like to make a controlled approach. I set this up by running out on a reciprocal of the close-hauled course to the line. Then I come back at the line hard on the wind. Though this method applies to both a port- and starboard-tack start there are some key differences in the way I make my approach.

With a starboard approach you have to work hard to win the spot right up at the committee-boat end. First, I try to stay away from the committee boat, because that keeps my competitors thinking I am going to start somewhere else on the line. When there are about ten minutes to go before the starting gun I make three timed approaches to the line, approaching the committee boat on port tack. When I am 50 yards to leeward of the committee boat, I tack quickly onto starboard, then sail close-hauled and cut the port corner of the committee boat's transom.

As I go through the three practice starts I determine the

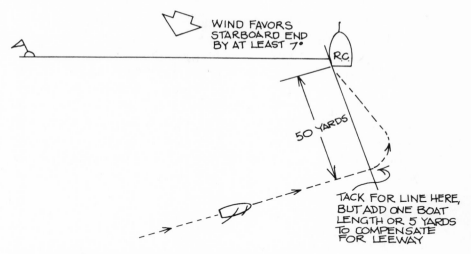

WIND FAVORS
STARBOARD END
BY AT LEAST 7°

R.C.

50 YARDS

TACK FOR LINE HERE,
BUT ADD ONE BOAT
LENGTH OR 5 YARDS
TO COMPENSATE
FOR LEEWAY

Fig. 6-3. Getting a good start using a starboard-tack approach requires good timing, as well as exact knowledge of where the transom of the committee boat is located. Make at least two practice approaches and try to memorize the angle made by the committee boat's stern so you recognize it when you make your final approach.

amount of time it takes to complete my approach. I study the angle of the committee boat so I have it firmly in mind. I also try to get a visual feel for how far to leeward I am from the boat. I keep all these elements in mind, so that when I tack for my final run to the start I can position my boat on its closehauled course within three feet of that committee boat's transom, or the mark, if one has been set. When I have those angles down exactly I add on an additional 5 yards to windward to cover any unexpected leeway (Fig. 6-3). Your timing must be perfect, and that is why you have to make those three practice runs. Your object is to keep anyone from getting inside you on your windward quarter.

Keep the boat moving, and use the racing rules to feather your way into that corner position. And as you sail into the corner, make sure the other boats around you are aware of your presence. Ideally you want to be ahead of, or at least perfectly even with, any boats just underneath you when the gun goes.

If there is about one minute to go and you can't locate the

exact spot where you should make your starboard tack to head for the line, your best move is to tack onto starboard a little early and get your boat going quickly. Then come up from behind and start squeezing up everyone who is to windward. If you can make one final head-to-wind move on those boats at the right moment—ten seconds or so before the gun—you may be able to get the 5-to-10 yard jump you are looking for, and you still may be able to start right on the corner. There is no question that this is a scary tactic. But every starting line is a little scary if you have fifty or more boats on it!

Also keep in mind that if there is a real tangle of starboard-tack boats as you sail up on port tack you are probably going to be better off if you start 50 to 75 yards below the committee boat. It's risky to tangle with a big crowd of boats like this, though it is true that once in a while, after you have tacked onto starboard, you can literally talk your way past boats by asking someone to "please head up," or "please head off." If you can talk some boat into heading up, you might squeeze by them to leeward, lay off, and go for the line.

As I've said before, you can tell a lot by watching how a skipper and crew handle their boat. Stay well clear of any crew who seem to be unsure of what they are doing. They could make a wrong move that results in a collision that could throw your strategy off as you jockey for position (even if you are later proved to be right). What you want to do at this point in the race is either win the start outright or be somewhere in the first tier of competitors and be close to where you want to be on the line.

As you make your final approach to the starting line on starboard, always sail whatever the boat to leeward of you will let you sail. If that boat heads off, you should head off. If it comes up, you have to come up as well, though you should try to be positioned so that you are slightly ahead of the boat to leeward when the gun finally goes off.

Port-Tack Start

This start takes good timing but, if you can master your

approach, often you will be successful in finding a good spot on the starting line. The reason is that as you approach the line on port, you are able to see all the potential holes that exist in the walls of boats sailing on starboard ahead of you and you can pick and choose which one of them you want to take. No one on a starboard tack really has this ability to maneuver over a wide range of headings.

Even if the port end is favored, don't think very hard about trying to port-tack the entire fleet. In a good fleet the odds are about 100:1 against you. Instead, pick a spot in the line of starboard tackers, sail up to that spot on port, and then tack over, get clean air, and accelerate away from the line on starboard. You must make a timed approach, and in order to do this correctly you should know the course you will be sailing on port tack as you head toward the line. Though you should already have this written down, it doesn't hurt to sail toward the line close-hauled on port to make sure it is correct.

My procedure for a port tack approach is to leave the line about two and a half minutes before the start; a good departure point usually is about one-third of the distance up the line from the pin end. Reach away from the line on the reciprocal of the close-hauled course for about one minute. Then swing around, tack, and come back on port hard on the wind. There is now about a minute and a half left to the gun, which means that you have built in about twenty extra seconds of time that you can use to position yourself properly with the boats coming at you on starboard.

Try to be between 50 and 100 yards away from the line when there is one minute to go, and make sure you position yourself on your final approach so that you are at least one boat length to leeward of the pin. If you are any closer, the mark is going to control your ability to maneuver if it becomes necessary (Fig. 6-4).

All the boats coming at you on starboard are going to be shaking their sails and floating slowly along the line. This is the great advantage of a port-tack start, for as you come in on port tack underneath them, you can see exactly how big all the holes are between the boats, and you can tell right away

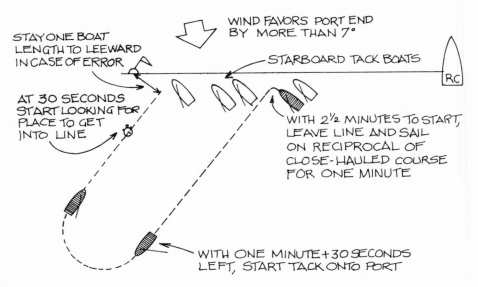

Fig. 6-4. One big advantage of the port-tack start is that it allows you to look for holes in the line, and gives you freedom to maneuver until just before the start. Leave thirty seconds for getting into the line, and keep a boat length between yourself and the mark.

whether you can get yourself into one of them. If you decide not to go for the pin, see where your biggest hole is down the line and head for it. If you do decide to try for the pin end and you reach it too soon and find yourself a premature starter, all you have to do is to quickly gybe around the pin, get yourself below the line, and go for another hole you have already spotted farther up the line.

Time things so you make your tack into the line onto starboard with thirty seconds to go. And if you want the pin position, don't let the starboard tacker closest to the mark know you are planning to tack underneath. Tack quickly onto starboard, stay on a very close-hauled course, and after you have given the other boat time to fulfill its obligation to keep clear of you, start your gentle squeeze to windward. Hail your intentions; that boat must respond to your movements. Ideally you will now be in a position to turn the entire fleet to windward. If you can, you will control the entire starting line.

With those few remaining seconds you can quickly lay off for the line, just as you would do on a starboard-tack approach, and hit the line at the gun. Once you head off, the other boats above you will do the same thing. But if you maneuver quickly you still should have a two-second jump on everyone else and be able to accelerate into clear air. This is why winning the pin end can be so worthwhile, and if the port-end favor is 10 degrees or more, I would try very hard to get that pin-end position.

But any time you try a port-tack start, you must always have a second and possibly a third move all ready to go in case you make a miscalculation. You can't ever afford to have the entire fleet run over the top of you on starboard tack after you have messed up a port-tack approach. It's not especially desirable to sit there bobbing in the water like a cork with your sails flapping and no other plays to make!

If you are early at the line, the best thing to do is to gybe around the mark and remember where the other holes in the line were located as you made your final port-tack approach.

Fig. 6-5. If you are over the line early, the best procedure is to come around slowly, tacking and then gybing so you come back at the line on port tack ready either to get back into the line or to break through and sail out to the right side of the course.

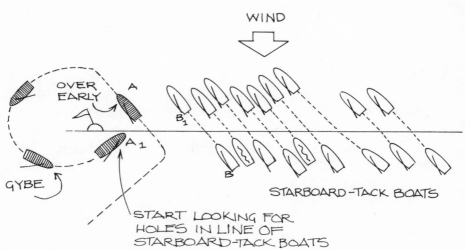

You can recover very quickly when you have a move like this planned in advance.

In fact, if you are over early in light-to-moderate winds, the best thing you can do is to make a gentle turn to keep speed up, and come back at the fleet on port tack (Fig. 6-5). Never try to spin around sharply and jamb right back up at the pin unless you are sure there is going to be a hole there. Instead, take aim a little further down the line and wait for your hole to appear in front of you.

This is one time when you need very good communication on board. As you gybe around, one of the crew should immediately drop down into the cockpit clear of the sails and look at the boats on starboard. They won't all be moving at the same speed: some will be pinched out and slowed; some boats may even have tacked over to port. These are the situations that give you holes you can sail right through and break out into the clear on the other side. If you can sail through the line of boats on port it will be just like raising the window-shade on a sunny morning: You'll be free and you'll be rolling!

Remember that as you sail on port toward a starboard tacker, you probably are sailing at twice its speed and you should always ask, "Would you like me to tack or may I go through?" If the crew that is hailed says nothing, tack right in front of that boat and, of course, destroy its forward motion with your backwind. Most of the good sailors, especially the younger ones, know this. They know what happens when a boat tacks ahead or just to leeward of them, and they will tell you to pass on through.

If you hail a boat, it must make a response. If it doesn't, you must honor its right-of-way position and, if the crossing is going to be at all close, you have to tack underneath the boat you have hailed to protect yourself from a protest. This must be done, even though your backwind will hurt that boat so badly that, in light-to-moderate conditions, it could cost that boat as many as twenty places right there in the first five minutes of the race. This will certainly be true if you have good speed as you approach your competitor on port tack.

If the port-end favor is 7 degrees or less, you should probably give away the ultimate pin end position and look for a hole somewhere along the lower third of the fleet coming at you on starboard.

Remember that while a port-tack start does give you considerable flexibility on your approach, when you get up to the line you only have two options: You can either tack to starboard underneath some boat and get into line, or you can build up your speed to break through the line on port tack and sail out to the other side. If something goes wrong with either strategy, there's no time left to ask yourself, "What do we do now?" You must always have your next move figured out—even before you make your first move.

Vanderbilt Start

First described by Commodore Vanderbilt many years ago, this method of going off the line is a timed starboard tack approach to the line. But here, you time your approach to the starting line from a point downwind. You sail away from the starting line to that point, turn back to the line on a close-hauled course, then trim your sails for maximum speed and hit the line going at full speed when the gun goes off. The trouble with this start is that you probably won't be able to get away with it in any fleet with more than thirty boats in it. I might try it, though, if there were fewer boats than that, and here is how I proceed.

I run down the starting line on port tack until I reach the spot on the line where I want to be at the gun. It is always in the upper one-third of the line. When I reach that spot, I turn away from the line and reach off, on port tack, on the reciprocal of what is going to be my close-hauled starboard-tack course. I try to leave the line for the run away when there are one hundred and fifty seconds (two and a half minutes) left. I run away from the line for a minute and five seconds (sixty-five seconds), which leaves me a minute and twenty-five seconds to the gun. After deducting the time it takes to tack, I have fifteen or twenty extra seconds for my maneuvering and I can speed up or slow down as I come back to the line.

If you are in a big fleet, it is a good idea to leave yourself

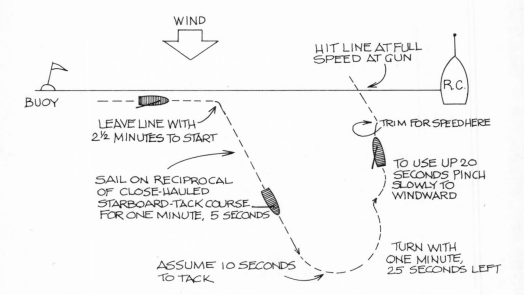

Fig. 6-6. The Vanderbilt start can work with small fleets, but good timing is critical. Build an extra twenty seconds into the return run to the line, then look for ways to avoid being over the line early.

twenty seconds, because all it takes is a couple of boats that are tangled up ahead of you to force you to go to your secondary move. You may even have to tack onto port to get yourself clear. So I make sure I have those extra seconds.

Once you are headed back toward the line on your close-hauled course, start getting yourself set up with your opponents nearby. The crew should be looking at the starting line and working on getting the sails set up for speed (Fig. 6-6). If you have twenty seconds to spare and nothing happens in front of you, you will sail back to the line at full speed and be over the line by twenty seconds when the gun goes off. So think about how to work off those seconds on your return. The best thing to do is slowly start heading up above the point on the line you have selected. This doesn't push the line farther away from you; in fact the mathematical distance between your boat and the line now is shorter. But pinching up like this does slow the boat down, and this is what consumes the time. Easing your sails out to slow yourself is another option, but this is far less precise and it makes it harder to accelerate again when you want to. With the pinching method, when you want to rebuild your speed, you merely head off onto your original close-hauled course.

Gate Start

The gate start is a good system to use in very large fleets, though I think at least four conventional starts should be tried first by a race committee. I feel this way because a gate start, or "rabbit" start, puts a big premium on boatspeed through the water. The first starboard tack away from the line is always going to be a very long tack. Even after the starting sequence is completed, you still are sailing off to the left side of the course on that long starboard tack, and that does favor the crews who have boatspeed.

If you are in a gate start, tactically what you want to do is pass just behind the transom of the guard boat moving along the line in front of you. This boat is located just to leeward of the boat sailing on port tack—the rabbit (Fig. 6-7). You should never be in a position where you have to turn your boat abruptly downwind to avoid a collision with the guard boat, and this can happen to you if you are being squeezed up by a boat to leeward of you. What often happens is that one boat starts luffing the boats to windward, then dives down and goes just astern of the guard boat. The way you guard against someone doing this to you is by carving a hole in exactly the same way you would on a conventional starting line.

The big difference, of course, is that once the rabbit has started to make its run across the starting area, you might not be able to cross its stern for thirty seconds or more, which could be how long it could take the rabbit to get over to you. This means you have a far longer period of time to spend protecting your position against the other boats around you in a gate start than you do in a conventional start. However, your main objective is to position yourself, when you finally do cross the stern of the guard boat, so you are sailing at top speed on a proper close-hauled course.

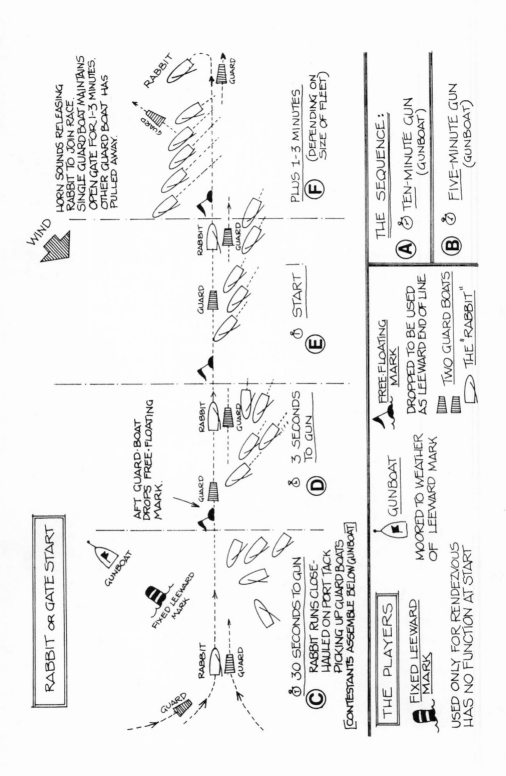

RABBIT or GATE START

WIND

HORN SOUNDS RELEASING RABBIT TO JOIN RACE. SINGLE GUARDBOAT MAINTAINS OPEN GATE FOR 1-3 MINUTES. OTHER GUARD BOAT HAS PULLED AWAY.

RABBIT

GUARD

GUARD

(F) PLUS 1-3 MINUTES (DEPENDING ON SIZE OF FLEET)

AFT GUARD-BOAT DROPS FREE-FLOATING MARK.

GUARD

RABBIT

GUARD

GUARD

RABBIT

GUARD

(E) START

(D) 3 SECONDS TO GUN

GUNBOAT

FIXED LEEWARD MARK

RABBIT

GUARD

GUARD

(C) 30 SECONDS TO GUN

RABBIT RUNS CLOSE-HAULED ON PORT TACK PICKING UP GUARD BOATS

CONTESTANTS ASSEMBLE BELOW GUNBOAT

THE SEQUENCE:

(A) 🕐 TEN-MINUTE GUN (GUNBOAT)

(B) 🕐 FIVE-MINUTE GUN (GUNBOAT)

🏴 FREE-FLOATING MARK

DROPPED TO BE USED AS LEEWARD END OF LINE

TWO GUARD BOATS THE "RABBIT"

⛴ GUNBOAT

MOORED TO WEATHER OF LEEWARD MARK

THE PLAYERS

FIXED LEEWARD MARK

USED ONLY FOR RENDEZVOUS AT START HAS NO FUNCTION AT START

Dip Start

A dip start, which involves sailing above the line and then dropping down below it just before the gun, is becoming less and less useful because in most good racing classes—for small boats as well as for ocean racers—everyone is moving slowly up to the line before the gun with their sails luffing. Then they are all trimming in and going together. This type of start leaves no room for someone who is trying to get down into the crowd from above the line. The risks of getting caught above the line are just too great for anyone who is serious about getting a good start. It does work occasionally, if the racing rules permit it (many races don't), but it is nevertheless becoming fairly obsolete.

Starting Strategies

In any competitive fleet your chance of making a comeback after a very bad start is small; that is why your maneuvering in the starting area is so important. Every line is going to be just a little bit different from the others, so working out a good plan ahead of time can help. But make sure that you have several alternate moves prepared, if your basic plan gets into difficulty.

And when you get in among the other boats and start heading for the starting line, don't raise your voice at the opposition. Handle your boat crisply and tell those around you what you expect them to do. You might tell the boat to windward of you to head up. But do it in a calm and clear voice. You might rap on the hull of your own boat for added emphasis.

In the final seconds before the gun, always sail whatever the boat to leeward of you will let you sail. If that boat heads off you should also head off. If it comes up, you have to come up as well. When the gun finally goes off, try to be slightly

Fig. 6-7 (opposite). In a gate start the thing to avoid is being forced up to windward and then having to turn downwind quickly to get across the line. For a good gate start, sail right behind the stern of the guard boat and be moving at full speed as you cross.

ahead of the boat to leeward of you and be moving at full
speed.

If you aren't over the line early at least one or two times a
year, you aren't getting up on that line as aggressively as you
should, though you always have to think about the penalties a
race committee might assess for early starters. Personally, I
would like to see race committees think hard about applying
a penalty after the first general recall. There would be no
penalty on the first start, but if there is a recall, the one-
minute rule would apply for the second. And if you are over
early on the third start, home you go! I remember a Star
World Championship in Marstrand, Sweden, where we had
perfect sailing conditions with 15 knots of breeze. But there
were fourteen general recalls, and we didn't even get in one
race!

THE WINDWARD LEG

Spend the first minute of the race working hard to get the
boat settled down and moving up to its maximum speed.
Basically you do this by moving your sail controls from the
power shape to the high-speed shape, and by keeping yourself
in air that is undisturbed by other boats. Build this speed up
and hold it for three to five minutes. And unless you are being
overwhelmed by a boat to windward, avoid making a tack
during this period. Every tack you make will result in the loss
of at least one boat length to any boat that is sailing a straight-
line course. Avoiding tacks is especially critical in light or
moderate conditions or in choppy water.

When you go over the line, the crew should be up on the
windward rail, or hiking out, and someone should be calling
the compass headings out. You, as skipper, should be adjusting
your helm and your sail trim for the higher speeds.

Concentrate on the oncoming waves so that one of them
doesn't sneak up and stop the boat cold. Look up the course
for the walls of wind moving down the course; analyze whether the anticipated oscillations will help or hurt. Always be
thinking about the original game plan you made before the

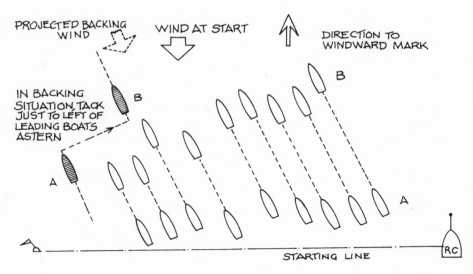

Fig. 6-8. To secure your lead over other boats, you should tack to consolidate your position at some point after the start. When you do sail back toward the center of the fleet, tack back just on the side of the fleet that you feel will be the favored one on the leg. Here you expect the wind to back, so stay just to the left of the leading boats in the middle of the fleet.

start. That plan was based on the wind readings you took before the start, and if there has been a change you must be able to modify your plan quickly.

At some point after the start, within two to five minutes, depending on the conditions, tack to consolidate your position with the fleet so that you can come up to the windward mark in at least the first seven places, and preferably the first three. To be successful at this you have to think about where your main competitors are, what you think the current is doing, and what you anticipate the wind direction will be. "Consolidate" means get over to the middle of the fleet and nail down your position. Staying at one end of the fleet always leaves you at the mercy of an unfavorable windshift.

If I happen to get the pin end at the start and there is a port-end favor, I work to windward as quickly as I can on starboard tack. I watch my compass for a slight header, and when the first opportunity comes to tack I do so and sail across the fleet on port to consolidate (Fig. 6-8). If I believe the wind is going to continue to back I will tack onto starboard again, staying just to the left side of the boats in the center of the fleet. This is called tacking and going with the flow.

If I think the wind is going to shift to the right, I will sail on until I am on the right side of the boats in the center. When I tack back at the center of the fleet, I am very careful always to stay on what I believe is going to be the favored side of the course. And I'll stay to that side seven-eighths of the distance to the windward mark.

The rules for consolidating are: get clear air first; then establish your speed supremacy over the boats around you; get settled down; and then start to watch. If you are on starboard tack at the leeward end of the line and you see boats above you to windward start to fall in to you, you are being headed and you should hold on. But if you see them start to lift away from you, that is the time to go over to the port tack and make your move to consolidate your lead.

However, if you come off the line on starboard tack at the windward end of the line and you find you are in a backing situation, you might want to tack onto port right away and go with the flow even though that tack does put you, for the moment anyway, over on the right side of the straight line to the windward mark rather than the left side, which is where the favor now lies.

Don't get too greedy right after the start. That is to say, make your consolidation tack as soon as you can. Sail back toward the center of the fleet, and tack back again to tie down the lead you have.

There is one excellent way to test how effective your consolidation tack has been. Let's assume I have gone off the line on starboard tack about one-third of the way up from the leeward end of the line. I have worked out nicely on starboard and now I want to tack onto port to consolidate my position. I go onto port tack and have sailed for about fifteen seconds when a competitor crosses my stern on starboard going to the left side of the course. I sail on for one more minute. Then, to consolidate my position again with the fleet, I tack back onto starboard. But wait a minute! Here comes my friend back at me on port tack, and it now appears that he will cross my bow by three boat lengths.

This can mean one of two things. The first is that my boat is very slow compared to my competitor's. If I can honestly answer that this just can't be the case, then I can proceed to the second possibility, which is that the left side of the course is paying off. But I want to test to be sure. So I continue to sail out to the left on starboard. Then I tack and take a new consolidation position that is a bit further to the left of the center of the fleet. But when I tack back onto port for my consolidation move, my compass shows me that I am sailing 3 to 4 degrees higher on port tack, and this is how my competitor picked up those three boat lengths.

Making this kind of check is a good way to reassure yourself that your compass isn't lying or that you aren't making a mistake about which side of the course the new wind is coming from. My extra tack proves to me my competitor has gained on me because the port side of the course *is* definitely favored. Therefore I now know I have to stay a bit more to the left side of the course than I had planned previously. You can use the same test to find out about the right side of the course. But this test can work only if your crew can spot a situation where you are going to cross someone. They remember the relative positions, and then make an interpretation the next time the two of you meet.

Testing the favor using another boat like this is also a good way to spot an unseen windshift without having to wait for your own compass to tell you about it. Obviously your compass *will* tell you about it, but it won't do so until you actually sail up to, or into, the new wind. If you can spot a boat like the one in this example, and keep track of how the two of you are crossing each other, you can often spot a shift like this well before you actually reach it.

The projected favor determines where you sail on your way

up the course. If I think the right-hand side of the course is
going to be favored, I stay just to the right (to windward) of
my competition. Whenever I tack, I always look at the boats
that are to weather and astern of me. I memorize their
locations relative to my boat. Then I sail with total concentration for several minutes and then recheck their positions. If a
boat that is well to windward when I tack is now sailing down
on me, there can be only two possible reasons: the other boat
is not being sailed well, or I am in a backing situation. But I
should already have been told that by my compass.

If the other boat is lifting away from me and I can't see it in
my compass, there are four possible explanations: the boat is
being sailed faster; it has a fresher wind; it has a current favor;
or, the wind is veering slightly. Whatever the case, my best
defense in this situation is to tack and get over into my
opponent's water as quickly as I can. If I have a four-boat-
length lead and I think the situation is due to either wind or
current, I will tack directly in front of the other boat. But if I
think the problem might be my own boatspeed, I will cross its
bow and then tack so I will give it turbulence off my sails.

You can sail to windward and make the correct tactical
decisions about when to tack, or not tack, by just looking
around at the other boats. Use them as reference points. If
you are on starboard tack with a boat ahead and to leeward of
you, and you slowly begin to slide down toward it, either you
haven't set your own boat up properly or both of you are
sailing into a backing wind and you are being headed. If you
begin to lift off the other boat, either your boat is well set up
and you are sailing better, or you both are moving into a
lifting windshift. Either solution may be correct, so stay alert
to both possibilities.

But always try to stay just to the favored, or windward, side
of the boats you feel you have to beat. If you are ahead of
them at this point in the race—after having made your consolidation tack—let the boat astern make the next move. Let
that boat decide which side of the course is favored. Your job
now is to make the correct response to those moves when
they come.

THE WINDWARD MARK

I don't think it is a good idea either to go out to a corner of the course or, when you get near the mark, to go to a layline. Making either move doesn't leave you any other options. The first windward leg always is a mass of boats sailing close to one another. Ideally you should be in a position to pick up the phasing sequences of a clocking and backing wind. The best circumstance would be to have a backing shift as you get near the windward mark on starboard tack, so you can come into the mark on port tack and avoid the big parade that always forms over on the starboard layline.

If you are somewhere in the middle of the fleet, you have to anticipate how the boats ahead of you are going to be coming into that windward mark. Then you must take those assumptions and put yourself in a spot where you are going to have clear air as you come up to the mark. If you have good air for the last 400 yards, you can often pick up as much as 200 yards on boats that don't have anything to sail in but turbulence.

Obviously, you have to work all the shifts as you go up the course—a 5-degree wind shift should make you think hard about tacking—but it is those last 50 yards to the mark that can mean as much as a 400-yard gain when you come out on the other side of the mark. This potential is especially significant in very large fleets.

While it certainly is a safe move to go over to the starboard layline and then tack, sail up, and go around the windward mark, the trouble is that a lot of other boats often have the same idea. It's very much like coming in at the starboard end of a starting line. And wherever there is congestion, there is confusion. If you do come up to the mark on starboard, someone is sure to sail in right ahead of you and tack to starboard right on top of you. If you make your tack far enough away from the mark, there could be any number of boats tacking to starboard in front of you, with each one driving you further out beyond the layline.

So the *worst* thing you can do is to establish yourself too early on the starboard layline. Every time you go out farther

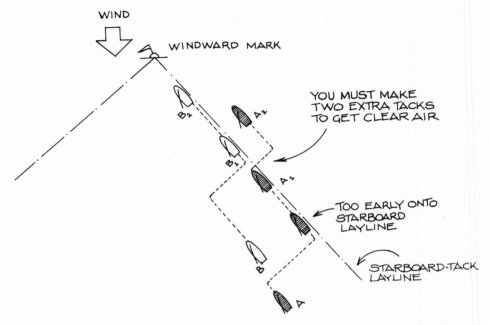

Fig. 6-9. Getting onto the starboard-tack layline too soon inevitably results in competitors sailing across on port tack and then tacking on top of you. The result is disturbed air, and you may have to make two more tacks to get clear of the turbulence.

to get clear air you have to make two more tacks—one to port to get clear air, the other back onto starboard. When you finally do get to the mark, you have lost many yards and probably several places. This will occur every time you go to the starboard layline too soon; you'll be buried in traffic (Fig. 6-9).

A far better plan is to come into the windward mark on port tack. In this maneuver you come in just as you do at the port end of the starting line. But here again, be sure to have a second move ready to go, in case something doesn't work out quite right. And just as at the start, now when you come in on port tack, you can see the line of starboard-tack boats ahead and to leeward of you and you can easily see all the holes in the parade where you might get into line.

Now is the moment when you should begin to think about

whether you ought to charge in or be conservative. If it appears that you are going to be early at the hole you have selected, this is the only time in the entire race that you should ease your sheets and either slow or stop your boat. But always maintain your course and let the parade of starboard tackers move up to you. Then trim your sails in, and tack into the line.

Never turn your boat downwind and go against the grain. If you do you will immediately lose your sense of how big the hole actually is, and the chances are good that both your main and jib are going to be overtrimmed. All of a sudden you'll find you have sailed a hundred yards *away* from the windward mark when only a minute or so earlier you were only two boat lengths away (Fig. 6-10). The reason is that it takes place all the time in sailboat races, and it is always the wrong move. So if you are early, let your sails out, slow down, and watch. Then, when the time is ripe, go right in on port, tack onto starboard, and go around the mark.

Fig. 6-10. A port-tack approach to the windward mark is often a desirable move. But if there is a fleet of boats on starboard, the correct move is to slow the boat down rather than heading off and sailing to leeward. If you do head off, you will lose distance and also have to swing the boat in a wider arc when you tack onto starboard.

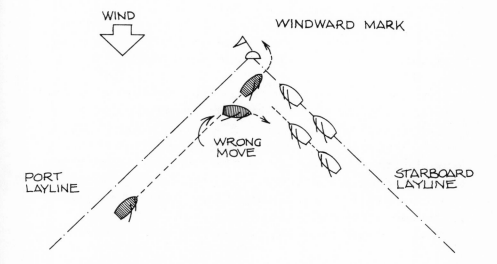

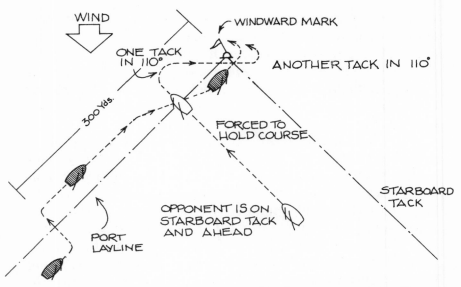

Fig. 6-11. One time it might pay to overstand is when an opponent is sailing on starboard. If you can force that boat to hold its course, it will have to button-hook, making two 110° tacks, and this can put you ahead at the mark.

Never come into the windward mark on port tack with it dead ahead of you. Always stay about one and a half boat lengths to leeward of the mark, because this gives you the room you might need for maneuvering. Now the mark can't dictate the movement of your tack. Always remember too that the turning point of any sailboat occurs at the keel, centerboard, or bilgeboard, and you want it to come around gradually instead of putting it into a speed-killing, sharp buttonhook turn.

There could be one time you might overstand the windward mark if you are thinking about a port-tack final approach. If you are sailing up to the mark on starboard and you have a competitor close aboard on your windward quarter, you might try sailing beyond your tacking point by a distance of one length. Then quickly tack your boat and try to pin the starboard tacker by making that skipper hold the starboard-tack course as you steer a course to just stay clear. This maneuver should carry your opponent perhaps two boat

lengths beyond the point where he is not overstanding. After
you have cleared the other boat's transom, you can harden up
and come to a course that is either right on, or just above, the
windward mark. Because you now are closer to the mark than
your opponent, the chances are excellent that you will be able
to break an overlap by the time you reach the windward
mark (Fig. 6-11).

At all other times, though, you should never come in hard
on the port layline. Always be just a bit shy of it, so that when
you get there you have room to roll into a gentle squeezing
tack around the mark. You can't afford to let the mark pin
you, which is what can happen if you are too close on your
approach.

If the left side of the course is favored, a lot of sailors make
the mistake of close-covering a boat on starboard tack and
forcing it to tack to port. You should give that boat freedom to
go over to the left side of the course, because that is where
you want to be (Fig. 6-12). As long as you keep a good cover
on your opponent using this guideline, there is little chance
that you will be driven off to the unfavored side.

If neither side of the course is favored and you want to
cover a boat astern, get yourself positioned so you have what
is called a perfect cover (Fig. 6-13). Once you are in that

*Fig. 6-12. When you are sailing on the wind to the unfavored side of the
course, be sure to provide a close cover. Doing so forces the boat astern to tack
and sail toward the favored side, which is where you want to go. At this point,
provide a loose cover so the boat will not have to tack and head back to the
unfavored side.*

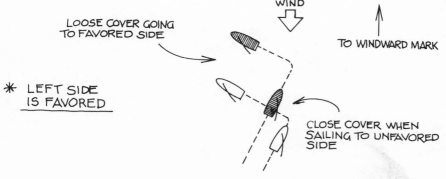

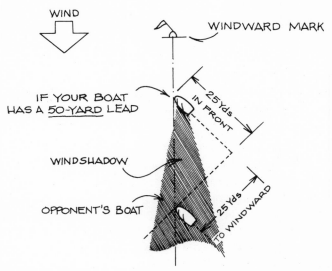

Fig. 6-13. A perfect cover on a boat astern keeps you in the control position even if the wind shifts. Position yourself so that you take half the distance of your lead to windward of the other boat and half the distance in front of the other boat.

Fig. 6-14. When you are approaching the port tack layline to the windward mark, pinch up slightly before you hit the layline. The distance you make to windward by pinching is translated into increased distance between you and your competitors when they tack astern to head for the mark.

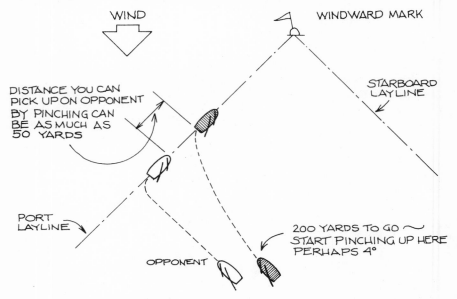

position, there is not much the other boat can do to get by you except sail through your wind shadow.

Though I said earlier that you should never go out to the port tack layline, there might be a time when it could pay to sail out that far. Current or tactical considerations might make it an attractive thing to do; if so, there is a maneuver you can institute that should pick up some extra yardage on the boat astern. In this case, if I do sail out to the port layline on starboard tack, when I get near the point where I want to tack over onto port, say around 200 yards away, I begin to squeeze up to windward. I might head up as much as 3 to 4 degrees above my close-hauled course as I pinch the boat up. If the boat astern of me stays on its close-hauled course, I may be able to pick up as much as 50 yards on that boat when I finally tack over onto port (Fig. 6-14).

THE REACH

Going around the windward mark I often see boats coming up to the mark, spinning right around it, then falling "into the well" as other boats sail right over the top of them. What those boats have done wrong is head off before their spinnakers are up and pulling, and before their other sails are trimmed for the reaching leg. They have lost all their apparent wind and, inevitably, they just stop. So never bear away onto a reach until you are ready to hoist the spinnaker. And even then you might think about holding high on your course to prevent a boat from sailing over the top of you. Never overlook the possibility that some boat underneath you may be luffing you up to prevent the same thing from happening to it.

I like to have the spinnaker pole positioned so that it makes a 90-degree angle with the headstay—at least to start. This opens the leech of the spinnaker and keeps it away from the underside of the mainsail, where it can choke off the slot.

I always like to have a telltale on the pole-topping lift so that the spinnaker sheet trimmer can see it. This location puts it right in line of sight and gives the crew a split-second

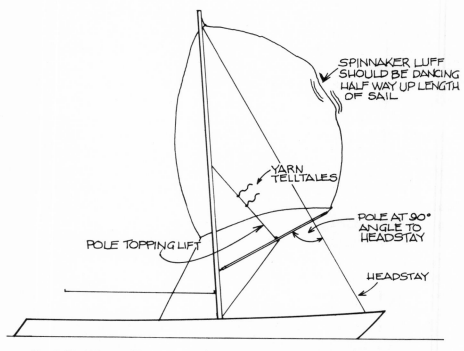

SPINNAKER LUFF
SHOULD BE DANCING
HALF WAY UP LENGTH
OF SAIL

YARN
TELLTALES

POLE AT 90°
ANGLE TO
HEADSTAY

POLE TOPPING LIFT

HEADSTAY

Fig. 6-15. When sailing on a reach with the spinnaker, start with the pole set at 90° to the headstay. Telltales attached to the pole-topping lift can give the spinnaker trimmer a quick way to see what the apparent wind is doing.

advantage in spotting a windshift that has taken place. The telltale should be kept at a 90-degree angle to the spinnaker pole, and the pole should be readjusted if necessary (Fig. 6-15).

If a spinnaker pole's outer end is carried too low for the wind conditions, the sail will luff first up at the head. If the pole is too high the sail will luff first down at the tack, and the entire spinnaker will have a tendency to oscillate and fall back behind the mainsail. If the luff of the spinnaker is dancing and fluttering in its midsection, this indicates a perfect trim. If the luff tape is not moving back and forth it is overtrimmed. The luff tape should be flip-flopping continuously.

If the sail does start to collapse, the helmsman must head

off quickly to keep it full. If the sail collapses easily the chances are good the pole is set too high and it should be lowered. If you are sailing on a close reach you should ease off the spinnaker halyard anywhere from 6 to 18 inches to get the sail away from the lee side of the mainsail, out where it can get good flow.

In keelboats the rate of opening and closing on a reach is slow enough so that it doesn't really pay to be overly aggressive going around the mark and to get yourself into a luffing situation where you can lose many places just to save yourself one place. For that reason I think it's far better to concentrate on getting a good spinnaker set and making sure all the mistakes happen on the other boats!

Once your spinnaker pole is ready, you should be able to get a spinnaker up and pulling in about four seconds. Don't have all the crew moving around the boat at the same time like bulls in a china shop. The skipper should be the only one to say *hoist*, because of the tactical situations that may be involved. Once the command has been given, the spinnaker should be pulled up as quickly as possible, using what I call a straight-arm overhead pull. To do this you grab the halyard down at the sheave and pull, with a straight arm, up over the head. This gives you maximum pull distance for each arm, and this can make a big difference in your haul-up time. Pulling with bent elbows is never as fast.

Once the spinnaker is up and pulling in a high-speed reach, it usually pays to move the crew aft. This raises the boat's forefoot and puts the flat sections aft down in the water for it to run on. You do have to be careful, though, if you are sailing a boat that has a deep forefoot. If the boat starts to heel over, that forward section can take over. If that happens, the boat can go into a broach very quickly.

Remember to check the compass course to the next mark as soon as possible after you come around the mark; make sure it conforms to the course you wrote down before the start.

The first reach of any race is much too early to get into a fight over position, so don't get carried away trying to luff up someone who is trying to overtake you to windward. Similarly, if you are the overtaking boat, don't insult the intelligence of the crew ahead of you by passing only 6 feet to windward of the boat's weather quarter. If you do, you are just asking for a response and you will certainly get one: a luff that can lose both of you many places before it is over.

If you do want to sail over someone, establish yourself high enough on your opponent's weather quarter and do so early enough so that when you do catch up and start to cast a wind shadow, that skipper will not turn and come up at you, because the required change of course will be so great, in terms of degrees, that there is no chance of catching you. Staying three to four boat lengths to windward should be enough to keep someone from coming up at you.

Whether you steer high or low of the base course to the reach mark depends on whether there is a current, what boats are around you, and what you think the wind is going to do. If you come around the windward mark first, let the boats

Fig. 6-16. On a reaching leg, holding high at first prevents other boats from sailing over the top of you. Going low on the second reaching leg can be the preferred course because of the improved wind angle when you are approaching the leeward mark.

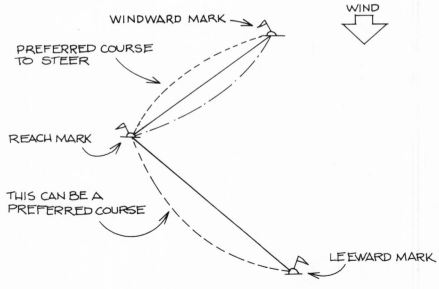

behind you make the first move (Fig. 6-16). Square away very slowly toward the reach mark and get all your sails pulling. In most cases any anticipated current gets too much emphasis too early in the leg. The fact is all boats can reach in current equally well, and any good sailor can alter course after proceeding down the reaching leg for as much as half the distance to the mark.

If you are behind the leaders going around the windward mark, what you need most on this leg is patience. Hound the boat directly in front of you and hope your spinnaker work is better, or that you'll figure out some way to get by the other boat before you approach the two-boat-length circle at the reach mark.

You have to work hard to keep your boatspeed up on a reach, and the first thing you should do is get the sails and rig set up properly. That really means building increased camber in the mainsail. You do this by easing off the outhaul, the cunningham, and the backstay if you have one. The only time you would not make these adjustments is in very heavy winds when you want the mainsail to remain very flat, set for the upwind position. Don't ease off the backstay in heavy winds, for that straightens the mast and puts the camber back in the forward part of the sail.

The boom vang and spinnaker sheet are the controls you use to keep your speed up on a reach. In fact the boom vang is the key to high-speed reaching. When a puff of wind comes, ease the vang quickly to unload the pressure buildup on the leech of the main before you go into a broach. Here is where a good deck layout helps you pick up places against your competition.

If someone has to come in from the rail and uncleat the vang, the boat will slow down. If you have a setup like this, you have already been beaten by a crew that can make these adjustments from out on the rail.

But as long as your boat remains under control you want as much vang tension as you can get. Only when the boat appears to be going into a broach should you ease the vang to depower the upper sections of the mainsail. If the broach continues, you must also ease off on the spinnaker sheet until you are under control again.

Once you feel a broach starting, the first thing to do is to pump the helm, and try to turn the boat downwind. The pumping motion—pulling the tiller first to windward, then easing it slightly, then pulling it again—should be rapid and continuous until you get back onto the course you want. The reason is that when you pump, you get far better flow attachment on the rudder blade than if you establish a fixed rudder angle and leave it there hoping that angle will get you past the broach. Once the boat does get back on its feet, pull your vang back down and get the mainsail back into its full power shape. And keep the hull of the boat sailing right under the rig.

The person tending the spinnaker sheet must concentrate exclusively on the luff of that sail, and the luff should always be right on the verge of breaking. If the pole is pulled too far to windward for the conditions, the spinnaker luff will collapse and the sail will have to be trimmed out with the sheet. But all this does is to hook the leech back into the main. Then the boat becomes crabby, and the minute a puff hits, it will start to heel over. So always keep the spinnaker pole well forward, and try to keep the spinnaker out ahead of you.

Be sure your sails are ventilating properly. If you know you don't have the reaching speed of some of your competitors, the only thing you can do is to stay high on the course at first, keep your apparent wind up, and hope you can hold onto your position until you reach the mark. Never let anyone sail over the top of you, because once that parade starts, it never ends! The only way to protect yourself against this is to plan to stay high of the base course as you come around the windward mark.

Planing

To reach successfully, you must use your apparent wind correctly, and to do this you must master the mystery of planing (if, that is, you are sailing a boat that is capable of getting up on a plane).

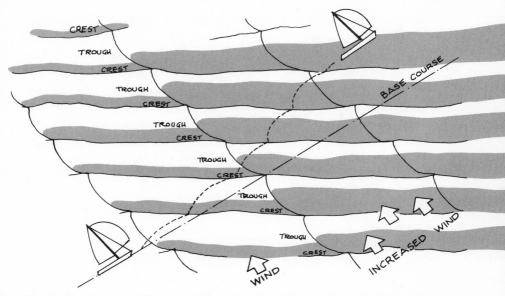

Fig. 6-17. When reaching through a band of increased wind, head off to maintain a constant apparent wind angle. In waves, head off the back of the wave but turn up quickly when you approach the front of the next wave. Turn downwind again at the crest to build up your speed. When you sail out of a wind band, head up again to keep your apparent wind angle constant.

If there has been no dramatic change in the wind direction since the start of the race, you can assume that the apparent wind is blowing at roughly a 90-degree angle to your heading. In iceboating when you are sailing with this apparent wind angle and the windward runner starts to lift and the boat heels, the correct thing to do is to head off immediately. When you do, your speed builds up dramatically. You do exactly the same thing in a sailboat, and if you can anticipate when these increased wind bands are going to arrive and time yourself to head off just as they hit, you will be much faster on this leg than competitors who don't know how to take advantage of the speed potential that is there.

As you enter a band of faster wind, you might be able to alter your course to leeward by as much as 15 to 20 degrees and still keep the same angle of apparent wind flowing over your sails. Steer so that you keep that apparent wind angle constant. To do this, you'll often find yourself making swooping arcs as the wind comes up and then goes down again. The idea is to remain in a wind band as long as you can, and if you do this properly you will probably find yourself to leeward of the base course to the mark. This shouldn't hurt you; if the wind starts to decrease you can head up toward the mark to maintain your apparent wind angle (Fig. 6-17).

Play your sails constantly and keep the boat right underneath the sails. If you start to get overpowered and the boat starts to heel to leeward, ease the vang off first. Ease the spinnaker sheet only when you are just about to go into a broach. Also keep the top sections of the jib in a soft or semistalled condition. Doing so keeps the sail the maximum distance away from the mainsail, and it also prevents the jib from sucking the spinnaker into its lee side.

If your boat can plane, break it out of the water as quickly as you can. Look astern for a wave that will give you a bit more momentum. As it catches the stern, head off quickly, and as the boat picks up speed, have the crew pump the sheets in and out, both spinnaker and mainsail, to give the boat some further assist. You can also grab the spinnaker guy and pull it back just as the boat is breaking through the crest of a wave. This pump can be very helpful in getting you over that crest and into a slide just a second sooner than you would have if you hadn't pumped. Once you are up on a plane, use the wind and the waves to keep your speed up.

One thing to watch closely when you start to plane is the action of the spinnaker. Very often, when you start to build up your speed, you will notice that the spinnaker sheet becomes almost slack because of the increased boatspeed and reduced apparent wind. While the natural response is to trim the spinnaker in, don't do it! In fact, the correct response is to keep the spinnaker sheet eased out, for that is the only way you can get the best out of that sail.

Sailing the Waves

Sailing the waves on a reach is another interesting exercise, and you can pick up a lot of distance if you play them

Fig. 6-18. When reaching in a centerboard boat, you can get maximum speed as well as the necessary control by having the board lowered just enough so the stern wake "crabs" to windward one or two degrees.

correctly. To get the best from an approaching wave, turn your boat down the front of a wave and run with it. Then, as you approach the back of the next wave, turn slightly to windward so you don't just plow into the wave and slow the boat down. This can be almost a repetitive motion as you go down the reaching leg: Turn up as you approach the back of a wave and then turn down once your bow goes over its top.

You must also keep looking astern at the waves that may be moving up on you, to see how they are going to hit your weather quarter. Adjust your helm so you are in the best position to take advantage of these following waves.

The more bubbles you can get under your hull on a reach, the faster you are going to be moving. But boat control is very important here, and there is a very fine line between skidding too much and not skidding at all. If you are sailing a center-board boat and you start to skid, and then get yourself broadside to the wind, you are going to wind up out of control and nature is going to take over!

Try to build up enough speed so that you can control the direction of the boat by body movements and perhaps just a very small amount of helm. If you have a centerboarder, you will have the best of both worlds—control and speed—if you pull the board up just to the point where, as you look aft, your wake is turning slightly to windward—no more than a degree or two (Fig. 6-18).

THE REACH MARK

If there are no boats to leeward of you, it is best if you stay high on your course as you come in to the reach mark. This will enable you to head down slowly as you go around, making a very gradual turn instead of coming straight in to the mark and then turning around it in a very sharp turn. In light or moderate wind conditions any sharp turn like this is going to slow you down considerably. As you go into your turn, keep the boat on an even keel (people will be moving around in the boat), watch your sails carefully, and keep track of where the wind is coming from. Watch the person handling the spinnaker pole and steer so that the gybing maneuver is made as easy as possible.

If it does happen that a number of boats are around you as you approach the mark, decide well ahead of time what is going to take place as you go around. You might, for example, decide to go straight in to the mark, do a very fast gybe, and come out on the inside of the turn to windward of the other boats. Or you could decide to make a slow and easy gybe and then run off to leeward. These options depend, to a large extent, on what the apparent wind is going to be on the next leg to the leeward mark. If the apparent wind has been relatively free on the first leg, the second reach will be much closer on the wind and therefore you should plan not to sail below the base course to the mark. But if the first reach has been quite a close one, the second reaching leg will be much freer, and you might give some serious thought to making a fake to the inside and then—when you have everyone start-ing to head up—breaking off and heading off to leeward. In any case, don't forget to recheck your compass course to the next mark as soon as you complete your gybe.

If you are still on your approach to the reach mark and you are just astern and to windward of another boat, there is a chance that you may be able to use the other boat's quarter wave to help propel you past it. This is a very good maneuver when you are sailing keelboats, for they can generate substan-tial quarterwaves. Position yourself so that you can catch the quarterwave and then, just as you do, turn your boat to windward very slightly so you are positioned to run directly down the face of those waves. This additional power is often enough to get you by. And even if your opponent decides at the last minute to head up and give you a luff, you should have built up so much speed that you can power on by if you have timed your move correctly.

Tactically, there is only one correct move at the reach mark—to get, and keep, an inside overlap. If you are ahead you'll want to prevent another boat from getting an inside overlap on you. And if you are behind you'll want to get an inside overlap on the boat ahead. If you are the trailing boat, one good way to do this is to stay right astern of your competi-tor and then make a feint to windward to get it to start up to windward to protect itself. But as soon as that boat starts its move, you break away quickly to leeward of the other boat and get that inside position. If you time your move correctly, when you have finished breaking off to leeward, both boats should be almost equal as you enter the two-boat-length cir-cle. With your inside overlap clearly established you can proceed to make a wide sweeping turn at the mark instead of gybing quickly around the mark and slowing the boat down. Another benefit of turning in a wide arc is that when you finally settle down on the new course your turn is going to put your opponent almost directly astern of you.

You may find yourself with several boats around you and, even though you are sailing faster, there is no way to get around them without getting yourself into a luffing situation.

One way to deal with this is to do a little variation on the
maneuver I've just discussed. In this case you head up to
windward and pretend that you want to sail by to windward.
As the other boats see what you are trying to do, they will
begin to head up with you, and the result will be that all the
boats below you will be sailing a higher course than they
normally would. At this point you suddenly head off and sail
straight for the mark. If you time this properly you should get
an overlap on all the other boats, just as you would with a
single boat (Fig. 6-19).

If you are defending your position against some boat approaching from astern, you should know how to defend yourself against an attempt to get the inside overlap. One good
tactic is to wait until you are about five boat lengths from the

Fig. 6-19. Getting an inside overlap at the reach mark often requires a move
like this one: Head up long enough to get the other boats to head up to protect
their windward position. Then head off suddenly and, when everyone else is
headed for the mark, you become the inside boat and get the overlap at the
two-boat-length circle, which gives you the right-of-way as you go around.

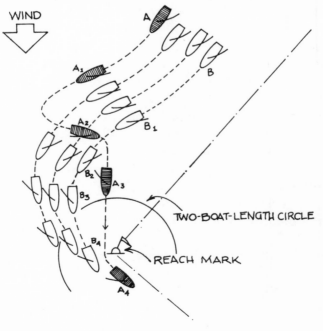

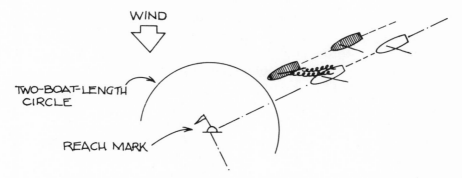

Fig. 6-20. One good way to keep a boat from trying to get inside you at the mark is to sheet in the mainsail so your boom is pointing at the tip of the other boat's boom. This disturbs the air flowing over the other boat's sails, and it should be sufficient to keep you in front as you enter the two-boat-length circle.

mark (possibly, in light air, as few as three lengths). When the boat astern tries to go below you to get the inside overlap, quickly pull in your mainsail so your boom points at the end of the other boat's boom. Even though you now are over-trimmed, this maneuver throws a lot of turbulence into the other boat's sails and it should discourage any hope your competitor has of getting that overlap on the inside. The great Star sailor Durwood Knowles taught me this lesson several years ago, and I have used it with great success ever since. If your timing is right, this one can be devastating (Fig. 6-20).

Snap Gybe

No matter how big or small your boat is, the biggest mistake you can make at the mark is to give the crew too little time to gybe the spinnaker exactly the way they have done it in practice. If, for example, you have never practiced a snap gybe—coming in fast, and then snapping the boat quickly onto the new gybe—then you should not try one in a race. And if you do get into trouble with your sails as you go around the mark, just try to sail the boat so that your crew can get themselves out of the difficulty. Basically this means sailing the boat so that the tangle doesn't get any worse. Trouble usually develops when the wind starts to blow over 15 knots. If your crew is having trouble getting the spinnaker pole reattached to the spinnaker guy after the gybe, you have got to sail a course that enables them to get that pole hooked up. If you don't sail that course, you are going to be in even more trouble later on.

A snap gybe, incidentally, is probably the best tactic for a crowded mark-rounding. With this gybe, you take the pole off the guy and attach it to the sheet on the leeward side, making sure the pole is pushed all the way forward to the tack of the spinnaker. Essentially, you are gybing the spinnaker before you gybe the mainsail. Now you are in a position where you can turn the boat quickly around the mark and either defend against another boat or go after a boat ahead of you. But even though you do turn the boat sharply in this maneuver, always try to steer so the sails stay right above the hull of the boat. If you get heeled over too far to one side, the force can quickly build up to the point where you won't have much steering control and your crew won't be able to work with any kind of efficiency.

Make sure the spinnaker is not overtrimmed after you come around the mark. This is a common problem, and the best way to avoid it is to look at the telltale on the spinnaker pole lift and adjust the pole so that it is 90 degrees to that telltale.

In heavy weather, you must take care to get around the mark without going into a broach. This is another situation where you should come into the mark well above the base course, then head off gradually as you start to make your turn, and finally position yourself so that you are running before the wind. In this case, you gybe the "back of the boat" first. In other words, gybe the mainsail before you gybe the spinnaker. Then, when the main is over on the new tack and things have settled down, go ahead and gybe the spinnaker, making sure you have the sheets muzzled down by the shrouds so the sail does not get over to one side of the boat.

You only alter your course about 30 degrees during a high-wind gybing maneuver—a lot less than the 90-degree course change you make if you come in to the mark at a sharp angle then turn around it quickly in a snap gybe.

In heavy winds you can get into trouble any time you gybe, even if you do head off very gradually to a downwind sailing direction. One way to stay out of trouble is to remember that as the boom starts to come over onto the new gybe, you should immediately steer the boat toward the direction the boom is traveling. "Follow the boom" is a good way to think of it. The reason you do this is to keep the boat under the sail and prevent it from going over on its side and into a broach.

Once a boat starts to heel to leeward, the boom can hit the water. If you have strong vang tension on the boom, that drives the boom further into the water, forcing the boat even further up into the wind, and a broach or capsize can easily follow. If you think you might get into trouble on the gybe, it is often a good idea to ease the vang off slightly before you gybe the mainsail. Once you are around you can retighten the vang and gybe the spinnaker.

If you do get into trouble at the reach mark, chances are it's because you have altered your course too sharply as you came around in the gybe. If you are in a small boat and you do capsize, remember that the spinnaker can easily wrap itself over the top of the mast and get in a terrible mess. Quickly assess the situation; if the boat looks as though it might turn turtle, get on the centerboard or bilge board and apply your weight to it to bring it back up. Other crewmembers should grab onto some sheets so that they can get maximum leverage high on the side of the hull to bring it back up. It's an excellent idea to get one crewmember up at the bow with his body extended down into the water as much as possible. This acts like a sea anchor and creates a lot of resistance to the wind and waves and tends to blow the transom downwind and keep the bow into the wind. Once the boat does get back up on its feet it will remain in a head-to-wind position as long as the person at the bow stays there. When the boat is upright, release the boom vang so the boom can rise and minimize the drive in the mainsail.

If you are in a centerboard boat, you can tip the boat over

on top of you if you don't have any board down as you gybe. Don't adjust your centerboard as you are going from one reach to the other. In all maneuvers, you must have enough board down for stability.

Going down the second reaching leg, your offensive and defensive moves are going to be just the same as they were on the first leg. As soon as you are around the gybe mark, start thinking how you are going to approach the leeward mark and how you are going to handle the boats around you. Plan how you can get an inside overlap to windward, or how to close your distance on the leaders. Avoid all luffing situations, because you can be taken right off the course by a defender. Stay far enough away from other boats so they won't have to attack you with a luff.

THE LEEWARD MARK

If you have been sailing smart enough to be leading the fleet as you come around the leeward mark and you have a large enough lead, you should utilize what is called a half-and-half. Basically you take half your lead in sailing distance ahead of your nearest competitor and the other half in getting to windward. Round the leeward mark smoothly and come close-hauled onto the wind, passing as close as possible to the mark. Once you are clear of the mark sail for two boat lengths. Then tack over onto starboard and sail close-hauled back toward your competitor coming down the reaching leg. When you feel that the second-place boat is either four lengths from the leeward mark or you have sailed half the distance of your lead up the course on starboard, tack onto port again so that both you and the other boat are on parallel courses as the other boat comes around the mark (Fig. 6-21). Though you have made two extra tacks you are now ready to defend yourself either by casting a wind shadow or by exercising tight defensive control.

At this point you should be reading the course headings you logged on the first weather leg and comparing any differ-

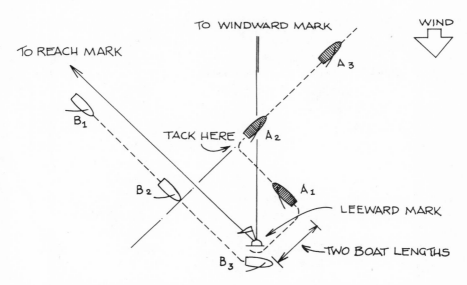

Fig. 6-21. The correct covering position to take at the leeward mark is to round the mark, go two boat lengths, then tack onto starboard and head back toward your opponent. When your bows cross, tack onto port and stay there until the other boat rounds the mark. This gives you a perfect position for covering the boat astern.

ences. Is the same side favored? If it is, you should also be able to figure out where the oscillations are going to occur as you go up the course.

If, for example, your compass tells you the left side of the course is favored, you must protect the left side of the course by keeping a loose cover on starboard tack and a very tight one on port tack. The idea is to encourage the boat astern to stay on starboard tack, since port is the favored tack. Maintaining a close cover on port tack should keep you ahead all the way to the windward mark.

That is the way to handle a single boat or even a group of boats that just follow the leader. Unfortunately, most of the time you aren't going to be as lucky. What usually happens is that the third-, fourth-, and fifth-place boats suddenly break out to the right side of the course, and they may even appear to pick up some wind. This is a typical racing situation, and you have to think everything through before you make your covering move. What is the correct thing to do now that there are several boats to the right of you? Here is where you have to start playing percentages.

Probably the best move, and a way to get the second-place boat astern of you to tack and come with you, is to tack over to parallel and consolidate your lead over the boats in third, fourth, and fifth places. You might also think about laying off onto the second-place boat, getting close enough to disturb its air, and making it tack over toward the other three boats. But that move shouldn't really be necessary, for the chances are good the second-place boat will go only a bit further on starboard anyway. Any conservative sailor would also tack and come after you and the other three boats. (This strategy could be different in dinghy racing, because there it is often faster to do a lot of straight-line sailing without making numerous tacks.)

If you are leading around a leeward mark, always let the boats astern of you make the first move, then react to them. Let *those* boats worry about which side of the course to go back up. The only things that might alter this rule are the compass headings for port and starboard tack you wrote down the first time you sailed up to the windward mark. You should know which side was favored on the first windward leg and what, if any, change in wind direction has occurred in the interim that would modify things this time up. These two things—the wind and the course favor for the first leg—along with any current effect, are all you need to keep track of as you let the boats astern determine where you are going to go. With this information you can plan your covering strategy.

If I am protecting on the second windward leg I let everyone else do my thinking for me, because in one-design sailing all the boats are pretty much alike and there isn't, or shouldn't be, any great magic in the speed differential between the boats themselves. The differences occur in the way the boats are handled by the skippers and crews. If a skipper pinches the boat up or lays it off, there is going to be a speed difference. If the skipper hasn't set the boat up the way it was set the first time up the windward leg, there probably is going to be some confusion. And that's why I always mark my sheets, backstay, and other adjustments once they are correctly set.

However, if I look at the headings written on the deck from the first windward leg and I see that one tack now is clearly favored, and the race committee hasn't made any course change to reflect that favor, this is the one time I would not throw a cover on the boats astern. Instead I would, after rounding the leeward mark, make a long tack on the *favored* tack to the next mark and take my full lead going out. The reason is that I might get an even bigger lift and actually fetch the mark. And even if I do get a header later on and have to bear off, so will my competitors astern and I will pick up even more. So if there is a big favor going to the windward mark, it does pay to forget about doing a half-and-half and go straight out on the favored tack.

If you are ahead, make the second windward leg the one where you protect your position. However, this is the leg where you are apt to get into a tacking duel with another boat astern—where all your training should pay great dividends. If you and your crew can quickly show the other boat you have superior tacking abilities, and every tack the other boat makes is going to cost it some ground, the attack will stop and you can again proceed with your straight-line sailing. The boat astern will give up if you can show your superiority immediately, and the next thing that will happen is that the second boat will begin to cover the third-place boat. Watch for this; when you see it happen you will know you can proceed to sail your own race and give the boat astern only a very loose cover.

If you are behind, in fifth place or worse for example, how can you pick up places on this leg? The best way is to never stop trying to get your boat set up correctly for maximum speed and never stop trying to put your boat just a little bit farther to the weather side of the expected favor than the boats ahead of you (Fig. 6-22).

Here's an example of what I mean. Sailing Stars in Sweden once, I was a hundred yards astern of another boat that was

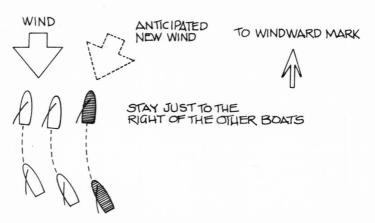

Fig. 6-22. On the windward leg, position yourself so you are on the inside of the anticipated windshift. If the wind is expected to go to the right, stay just to the right of the other boats. If it is expected to go to the left, keep your boat just to the left of your competition.

sailed by a former world champion. Both of us were on starboard tack going toward what was the unfavored side of the course. We both started to get a little lift, and this put my boat up off my opponent's starboard quarter. At that moment Andreas Josenhans, my crew, remarked that this was the highest starboard tack course we had sailed all day. Just then the other boat tacked onto port to protect its lead, crossed us, and tacked again to starboard right to weather of us. At that moment we got a small header and I tacked away to port. We were now only three boat lengths astern of the other boat instead of a hundred yards. Andreas informed me that we were sailing the average port tack course for the day. We sailed on port until we ran into another small header and tacked onto starboard again. The other boat came up on port, trying to cross us again, but we were sailing on a high starboard this time and we crossed ahead, and stayed ahead for the rest of the race.

How did we get by a boat that was so far in front? The answer is that Andreas was right on top of our compass headings, he was analyzing how we were moving across the real estate, and he was computing how long we should stay on a tack. Our tacking procedures were good, and because of our earlier readings we knew we could read the shifts correctly. This is why we stayed in close, trying to pick up small pieces of distance on the shifts instead of heading out to a corner and trying to pick up a mile.

Never be satisfied with your fleet position unless you are first. If you are in fifth place, try to force the fourth, third, and second boats into tight quarters with each other. When that happens you might somehow get around all of them, and break into the clear for your move against the lead boat. But you can't make *any* moves unless you think about them first.

The windward mark probably will be less congested the second time around. But you should still make your approach well inside the laylines and avoid getting onto the starboard-tack layline too early. Making a port-tack approach, just like the first time around, is a perfectly good procedure, but make sure you allow enough time on starboard tack to set up for a good spinnaker hoist.

THE DOWNWIND LEG

The critical factor for all downwind legs is whether the wind is in a veered or a backed position relative to the leeward mark. How you read the situation determines which gybe you are going to take after you go around the mark. If the starboard tack is the favored one to be on going into the windward mark, the wind has veered and therefore the port tack is going to be the favored one downwind. If the wind is blowing straight down the course, the best move is to make a starboard-tack set, get the boat under control quickly, release cunninghams and outhauls, and get the mast as far forward as you can for good downwind performance.

Under no circumstances, however, should you head your boat straight downwind after rounding the mark. If you do this in light air, your boat will stop in about three lengths. If the wind is under 10 knots, it is much better to go around the mark as though you were going to head off on a reach, get the spinnaker up, keep your speed up, and then start to pull the pole back as you slowly head off. But always maintain your speed. Keep heading off until you get down to the course you think will be correct for the velocity of the wind. The stronger the wind, the more directly downwind you can sail. The lighter the wind, the more you will have to head up to keep the apparent wind flowing across and ventilating your sails.

One quick way to keep your orientation on a light-air run dead downwind is to take the course to the leeward mark and then add 45 degrees to it. Use this course to set up your spinnaker gear, and come to that course as you move away from the weather mark. You may be able to head downwind even more if the wind increases. But sailing an initial 135-degree angle from the eye of the wind is a good place to start whenever you are sailing in light air.

Try and keep your boat square to the waves, and if there is any wind at all, try to promote a surf by pulling on both the spinnaker guy and the mainsail sheet just as you go over the top of a wave. Pull only when the spinnaker guy and the mainsheet are still hard to pull back. If the sheet and guy come back easily, the boat has already broken loose, is surfing, and you want those sails back out again quickly. If the waves are big enough it may even pay to sail by the lee as long as you can surf over a greater distance by doing so. But you must be prepared to break again to windward quickly and go up across the back of the next wave so you can get to the top quickly. Then, head off for another ride! But never sail by the lee except in these special sea conditions.

In fact, the only time you should sail by the lee is when you have broken loose, you are sliding down a wave, and you are powered not as much by the sails as you are by the force of the wave. This kind of sailing takes aggressive steering and aggressive sail-handling to start and maintain a surf. Consistent pumping of your sails is going to attract attention, and a protest. But if you pump methodically to get yourself started on a plane, and you do it in harmony with the wave action around you, that is acceptable under the rules.

If you are protecting your position downwind, always position your boat so you are a little bit to leeward of your competitor astern. This is another case where the other boat's masthead fly comes in handy. If you keep your boat inside the direction the fly is pointing, that keeps its wind shadow from affecting you. If the other boat starts to head up, you should head up an equal amount. However, be sure to stay between the boats astern of you and the next mark, and never let a boat get so far away from you that it might pick up some wind of its own. Instruct one of the crew to keep looking aft to see where the next puff of wind is coming from. If it is necessary to gybe to get over to a puff, do so quickly, for that is the only way you can be sure you can protect your position.

The reason to stay just a bit to leeward of a boat astern of you is that whenever you sharpen, or decrease, your angle to the wind it produces a faster course, and that means you can come up to protect your position if you have to. If you are to windward of an opponent all you can do is to head farther off the wind, which produces a slower course. You may even have to gybe. In either case you no longer have the potential to create a higher apparent wind speed relative to your opponent and therefore you have lost your positive control on the boat astern. So stay slightly to leeward at all times (Fig. 6-23).

Fig. 6-23. The correct covering position in downwind sailing is to leeward of the competition astern. This position allows you to head up, if necessary, to increase apparent wind and boatspeed. If you are positioned to windward of your competitor, your only covering alternative is to head off, which slows down the apparent wind, and your speed.

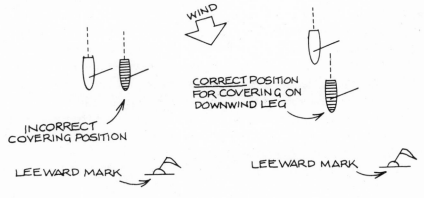

WIND

CORRECT POSITION
FOR COVERING ON
DOWNWIND LEG

INCORRECT
COVERING POSITION

LEEWARD MARK

LEEWARD MARK

When I first started racing in the Soling fleet, nobody was gybing downwind very much. Then the other boats saw me gybing all the time, and when they found I had a big lead at the leeward mark, everyone started doing it. And they all went a lot faster as a result. Unless the wind is blowing so hard that you are sailing at hull-speed, you are going to get to the leeward mark faster by gybing downwind.

And when you are gybing, you have to be the master of the art of ventilating. This technique, designed to keep the air moving across your sails, is one of the most important tactics for the downwind leg, yet it is often neglected, even by some very good sailors. Ventilation is especially critical in light-to-moderate winds. Big-boat sailors like to use tacking angles and break-even speeds to calculate all this, but the point is that if you can build your apparent wind up by coming a little closer to the wind, you can go considerably faster toward the downwind mark than you can by sailing square to the wind— even though you are sailing a greater distance. You do have to trim in your sails, for any time you come up as much as 30 degrees from the dead downwind course you will be on a broad reach. But in light air you can often double your speed by sailing this high. Because the speed of the boat has increased, the apparent wind speed will also increase and its angle will move toward the bow.

Now you can start to head off down toward your original course and still maintain the speed you have built up. Even though your spinnaker pole may be set at only a 45-degree angle to the boat's centerline, you can often sail a course that almost parallels the course of a boat that has made no move to come up on the wind. But that boat will be sailing slowly, almost dead downwind, with its pole pulled back to make a 90-degree angle with the centerline. Very often you can be going as much as four times the speed of the other boat because you are ventilating your sails: you are keeping the airflow moving faster over your sails than the air that is going across your competitor's sails. And you are moving faster through the water because of it.

Basically ventilation is accomplished by steering a scalloping course in much the same way you do on a reach. First head up onto the wind to build up the apparent wind over the sails and, when you have increased your speed through the water, start to head off away from your reaching course. As you head off, ease the spinnaker sheet a bit to open up the slot between the main and the spinnaker, but do not pull the pole back.

You will be able to maintain this speed for some time, but eventually the reduced apparent wind will start to have an effect and you will start to slow down. The minute your speed does begin to drop, you should begin to head up again, trimming in the sheets as you do, and gradually build up the apparent wind flowing over the sails. This in turn will get your speed back up and you can begin to head off toward the leeward mark again.

Heading off toward the mark can also be timed with an approaching puff of wind. But if the wind speed does increase in a puff, you now can bring the spinnaker pole back in addition to easing off the sheet. Watch your telltales to see where the wind is coming from, and be constantly alert to which tack is the favored one to the leeward mark.

One other element can influence your downwind legs—the angle of the waves relative to the course you are sailing. If you can use the waves along with the proper apparent wind angle, you will be able to get even more momentum. But if the waves are not a big speed producer, always sail whichever tack has the wind blowing farthest forward relative to the leeward mark. In other words, whatever tack to the mark permits you to sail more close-hauled is the one you want to be on.

You also must determine which is going to be the favored side of the course for the downwind leg. One rule of thumb is that whichever side was the favored one beating up to the mark is going to be the unfavored one sailing downwind. In other words, if the right side of the course was favored beating up to the mark, the left side should be favored on the run.

I know this is an old wives' tale, but it has worked for me on more than one occasion and it certainly is as good a place to begin your analysis as any I know.

Another good way to spot the favored side is to pick a boat that is sailing straight downwind to the leeward mark—somebody always does. Reach off on the starboard tack (actually either tack will do) until you have gone perhaps 150 to 200 yards away from the rhumb-line course to the leeward mark. Now gybe and come back on the port tack using the same *apparent* wind angle. As you cross the downwind rhumb-line course, you will be able to see whether you have gained or lost on the boat that has been going straight down the line. If you have lost but you still believe ventilating your sails is going to be faster than running straight downwind in the conditions, continue out on port to the other side of the course and go out the same distance. Then gybe and come back in again. This time you should find that you have definitely gained on the other boat. Instead of continuing over to the other side, gybe back onto port on the rhumb line and keep the same apparent wind angle as you once again go out to the side you now know is faster.

Never lose track of the wind direction and of any shafts of increased wind speed that are moving down the course. When they do hit you head off, pull your pole back, and ride them for all they are worth. When you have run through one, head up slightly, ease the pole toward the headstay, and start to ventilate your sails again.

If a gust does hit while you are moving through the water on a freshened or more close-hauled course, you can really make this pay because you will already have your speed built up, and now you can head off and go even faster. Contrast this with a boat that is sailing square to the wind and is hit with the same puff of wind. It takes that boat a long time to build up the amount of energy, as it sails on a flat run, that can equal the speed of a ventilated boat sailing a much closer course in higher apparent wind. That is the great advantage when you use apparent wind angle to ventilate your sails.

Even if you do a lot of gybing on the downwind leg, you should plan to come into the leeward mark on the headed tack. This could be the port tack, of course, and I wouldn't mind coming into the leeward mark on even a fairly close-hauled port tack. And this is true even if there is another boat near me that is running directly downwind on starboard. The reason I don't mind this kind of situation is that I am probably going to be moving at perhaps twice the speed of the other boat. And even though we are going to come together, when I get near the mark I can turn my boat downwind quickly, I can more than match the other boat's speed through the water and therefore I can move out in front of it before we get to the two-boat-length circle.

In heavy air, downwind sailing becomes a matter of good sail control rather than ventilation. Keep the spinnaker under tight control by muzzling it down; don't let it get way out in front of the boat. Flatten it in toward the bow as much as possible and keep it as flat as you can for the greatest amount of lift. Maintain a lot of boom vang tension to keep the mainsail leech standing up and to avoid twist at the top of the mainsail, which increases the potential for rolling. In more moderate conditions it doesn't hurt to heel the boat to windward just a little. This heeling gets more sail area up in the air, should eliminate any tendency toward having a weather helm, and in many boat types also reduces wetted surface, which can have a big effect on boat speed.

Going into the leeward mark, I always plan to make my last gybe so I come in at *least* three boat lengths to windward of the mark. Never make your final gybe so you wind up heading below the mark and have to head up. This is the same tactical mistake as overstanding on the weather leg. In both cases you lose yardage to your competition.

When you are about a hundred yards away from the mark, you have to be aware of all your potential overlapping situations. Always know where your opponents are relative to *your transom*, for the racing rules say it is the square off the transom that determines whether they have an overlap, and

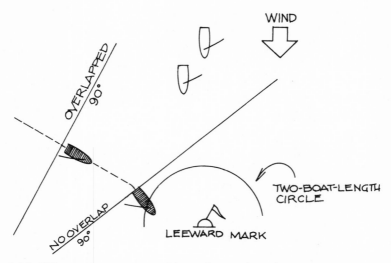

Fig. 6-24. When you are approaching a leeward mark, note the angle your transom makes relative to your opponent. A boat sailing directly downwind may have an overlap based on transom angles. But a boat that comes in at an angle and then changes course at the two-boat-length circle can break the overlap and therefore does not have to give an opponent buoy room going around the mark.

not whether you are the first one inside the two-boat circle (Fig. 6-24).

This is also a good time to consider attempting what we call on our boat a "Bertrand" (named for the famous Australian sailor John Bertrand, who is an expert at this maneuver). It is an excellent offensive tactic that can get you an inside spot at the leeward mark—if you do it properly. You have to set yourself up to do a Bertrand well before you get to the two-boat circle. Approach your opponent's boat on a fairly close angle of sail, cross its stern, and gybe over when you are between the boat and the mark. Because you have been sailing a more close-hauled course and your sails have been ventilating more, your boatspeed is going to be much greater and you can use that speed to float by on the inside, and get that inside overlap (Fig. 6-25).

Another tactic to use going into the leeward mark, or any mark for that matter, is to apply as much faking action as you can. Try to make all the boats just ahead of you think you are going to do something you aren't planning to do. For example, if you are actually planning to sail outside a boat at the leeward mark, pretend that you are going to try for an inside overlap. When you are perhaps four to five boat lengths away from the mark, sail in close to the stern of the other boat and make it appear as though you are going to try to force your way in between it and the mark. The skipper will head up toward you and tell you there is no room. As soon as that skipper moves the helm to bring the boat closer to the mark (theoretically to shut you out of the inside position), suddenly put your helm down and swing wide to the outside, across the other boat's stern. Now the other boat is trapped in close to the mark and can't possibly make a gentle turn around it. Instead that skipper has to jam the helm around, which turns the keel or centerboard quickly 90 degrees through the water, slowing the boat way down. Meanwhile you can sail around the mark on the outside, make a gentle turn onto the wind, keep the power on throughout your turn, and sail right

Fig. 6-25. Building up apparent wind and boatspeed can often be a very potent offensive move. With greatly increased speed you can sail across the stern of a boat, turn down to leeward, and because of high relative speed, get an inside overlap at the two-boat-length circle.

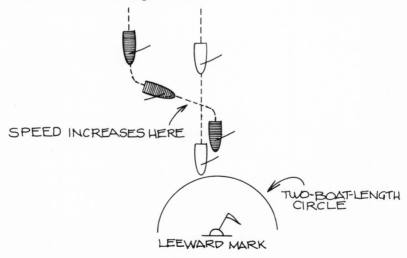

on through the other boat to leeward. Now you can disturb the boat to windward, because you are in the safe leeward position. The result should be that the other boat will have to tack away from you and go onto the starboard tack.

I prefer a spinnaker takedown to windward on the downwind run because I think it not only pulls the boat into the spinnaker and produces a bit more drive, but it also reduces the chance of a mess if the sail decides to turn inside out and flail off to leeward. The windward takedown does work well, it has no effect on drag, and even if there is a mistake, you can still round with the spinnaker blowing into the jib and it won't hurt you half as much as if it were streaming out to leeward in a beautiful hourglass. It's a good maneuver for dinghies and one-designs. And I am not sure that some of the bigger boats wouldn't also benefit from this maneuver.

Once you are around the leeward mark, don't tack back up into the fleet that is approaching you to windward any more than is necessary. If you are ahead and want to cover the boats astern, this is where you might think about sailing the distance of your lead out on port, and tack onto starboard only when your opponent tacks onto starboard after going around the mark. However, you do have to be prepared for the boat astern of you to make a slam starboard tack around the mark to try and get away even though it may mean sailing right into the fleet headed downwind. If this does happen the best thing to do is to tack and foot off to get in front of the other boat. Then put a hard cover on it.

A more conservative and safer way to protect your position is to sail half the distance of your lead out on the port tack, go over onto starboard for a quarter of the remaining lead distance, then tack back to port and get ready to make that next tack onto starboard. This maneuver gets you several boat lengths up the course to windward, even though it does get you a bit to the right side. Still, you must be aware of what the rest of the boats sailing down to the leeward mark are doing, and always try to keep clear of them. If you don't, you are going to be sailing in bands of disturbed wind.

THE FINISH

The beat to the finish line requires, like the previous beat, a very tough cover on the boats behind if you are ahead, and an aggressive set of offensive moves if you want to move up in the fleet. If you are in a regatta or series, this is the time to think about your point score. If a boat is right behind you and you want to get another boat between the two of you to increase your point difference, see whether you can get a third boat in ahead of your opponent. Doing this usually involves keeping a close cover on both port and starboard tacks to allow a third boat to come up. Never stop thinking about the final results in the regatta.

If you are ahead and going for the finish line, protect your position from directly in front of your opponent. The ideal cover always is half your distance up the course and half ahead of the other boat. You can use a safe leeward position, but plan your safe leeward tacks so they force the other boat to tack to the unfavored side of the course. After sailing two legs you certainly should know which side this is. The way to protect the favored side is to stay just to the windward side of your opponent. If the right side of the course is the favored side, stay just to the right of the other boats; if the left side is favored, stay just to the left.

If you are behind, you must ask yourself, "Is there any move I can make that will get me past a few boats before I cross the line?" Can you, for example, use your wind shadow to force other boats together so that you can break away at some point, get clear wind, and possibly even get the favored tack to the finish line?

If you are trying to come from behind on this final beat, the only way you can pass a boat is to go just a bit further out to one side of the course than the boats ahead of you and hope the wind shifts in your favor. Watch the oscillations by constantly reading your compass. Look at all the port and starboard courses you have recorded on the first two legs, and go to the side of the course that this history says is the correct

one. How far over to one side you should go is a decision you'll
have to base on your intuitions. You must protect your own
position over the boats astern of you, but you also want to pick
up some ground on the boats ahead of you. My own feeling is
that you should never be so aggressive that you go so far to
one side of the course and lose four or five boats in the
process. If I am trying to pick up some positions, I stay with
the general movement of the fleet but I try to get just to
windward of my competition on the side I think will be the
favored one. I want to be on the inside of the wheel when it
turns with a windshift.

Looking at it from the other side, if I am defending I try to
keep my position just to windward of all the other boats. If,
for example, I believe the wind is going to shift to the right
and someone is coming up behind me, I would produce a
very hard cover anytime I am on port tack heading to the
right side and I would force that boat to tack onto starboard. I
would give the boat freedom to keep sailing on the starboard
tack, because as long as it stays on starboard tack it will
continue to be downwind of my own position and won't be a
threat to me because I am going to be on the inside of the
shift.

Though it is not easy to do from a great distance, you must
begin to calculate which end of the finish line is favored.
Before you start making your observations, though, remember that the left, or pin, end of the line is the *actual* windward
mark. This means that any time you can fetch that mark, even
if you are a mile away, you should tack for it. Obviously, it is
tough to figure out what the exact favor on the finish line may
be if you are a mile to leeward. What you really have to do is
to sail up to the triangle created by the finish-line laylines
before you can determine the exact favor.

Once you are near the triangle, you can see more clearly
whether the finish line is square to the wind. If the line is
square, then both port and starboard laylines are equal and it
is simply a question of deciding which end of the line you can
fetch first, and tacking for that end as soon as you can. Every
foot you sail beyond the layline is wasted because you will be

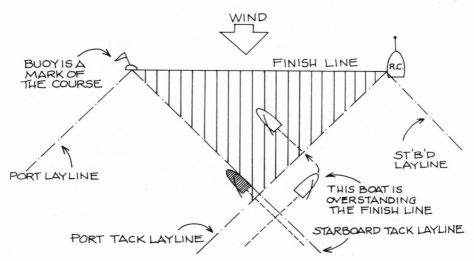

WIND

BUOY IS A
MARK OF
THE COURSE

FINISH LINE

R.C.

ST'B'D
LAYLINE

PORT LAYLINE

THIS BOAT IS
OVERSTANDING
THE FINISH LINE

PORT TACK LAYLINE

STARBOARD TACK LAYLINE

Fig. 6-26. The key to making a successful finish is to cross the line at one end or the other. Consider the laylines that extend from both ends of the line and tack for them. Unless there is a major windshift, stay out of the shaded area, because you would be sailing a greater distance to cross the line than is necessary.

overstanding the mark (Fig. 6-26). If, for example, you are approaching the finish line and you see that the favor is clearly at the pin end, you should tack onto starboard the moment you can fetch the pin. If you do not tack at this point, you are overstanding the finish line.

The best way to tell whether there has been a shift on the line is to look at flags on boats around the finish, and look hard at the flags on the committee boat. Also, another boat may be way above the line and sailing along on a much higher angle than you have seen all day. Look for these clues, for they are the telltales that can give you an idea about how the line is set. If you keep your eyes peeled you can often spot them when you are a considerable distance to leeward of the line.

Here's another thought you might keep in mind: If the race committee sets their starting lines with a starboard-tack favor, it's possible that you will find the same type of favor there at the finish line, even though the committee tries very hard to make it square.

From this discussion it should be obvious that you never should deliberately cross the finish line in its center. People do it all the time, but the fact is that they have overstood one of the laylines that exist at both ends of the line. So as you approach the finish, try to commit yourself to a crossing that will take place at one end of the line. Very often you won't be able to tell which end is favored until you get into the last hundred yards of the race and you are moving up in front of the line. At some point, though, you should be able to tell for sure which end is the favored one.

If you are heading for the wrong end it might be too late to do anything about it. But if you keep looking you might be able to capitalize on this last bit of knowledge and get across the line ahead of someone who has missed it. In any case, once you have made your decision about which end of the line to head for, go to that layline. And when you are there, tack for the finish and sail to it as fast as you can.

Never stop racing until you have crossed the finish line, because often you can pick up places right on the line. Jack Shethar taught me that in our Mallory Cup campaigns when, in one race, he took us from fourth to first in just the last few yards. In fact I had sort of resigned myself to taking fourth, but Jack wasn't at all interested in that score. He said we could win and he proceeded to put us in a perfect tactical position for our run to the finish. We were sailing up to the line on port tack, but Jack saw that starboard tack seemed to be the favored one, and he called our tack onto starboard perfectly. He positioned us so the three boats ahead of us were all on port tack and when we tacked onto starboard one of the boats had to duck underneath our stern, and the other two kept on going on port. But we beat them to the line simply because we were on the favored tack. Jack could see all this as we approached the line. He planned all our moves, then put us where we could carry out that plan. It was one of the most exciting finishes I've ever been in, with the first four boats separated by only fractions of seconds.

Another reason we won the race was that once we had

been shown what was possible, we decided we were going to keep working hard right up to the finish. No one was going to get across that line ahead of us if we had anything to say about it! And sure enough, no one was there to keep us from that first-place gun. We had sailed smart, and it had paid off.

7

REFLECTIONS ON WINNING

CREATING THE GOLD-PLATED PROGRAM

When I was just learning to race, my father kept saying to me, "Son, if you want to do well in this sport, be first at the start, stay out in front, and increase your lead." Well, that might sound like an oversimplification, but truer words were never spoken. If you *can* start first, it always is easier to stay at the front of the pack. And it is a whole lot easier to keep your lead than if you start back in the third tier of boats and then have to work your way through a bunch of sailors who don't want you to sail by them.

Sailboat racing becomes a game of chance only when you are not prepared. While there may be an unpredicted windshift or someone who gets an overlap on you when you aren't ready, in most fleets only the sailors who know they are slower than the rest sail out to a corner looking for that race-winning shift. If you deal with averages, going out to the layline on a beat to windward may win you a race, but it will never win you a series. Look at the best sailors and you never find them out on a corner of the course. They may go a bit to one side as they go up the first windward leg, but they never will go all the way out. I can think of any number of races where, if I had gone farther out on one side of the course on the beat up to the mark, I could have rounded it with a big lead. But this is something I do not want to do. It's not smart sailing! In a big fleet, any position that is among the first eight boats at the first windward mark is enough to make a good sailor reasonably happy. Then these sailors begin to work very hard to pick up some more ground on the downwind legs.

When you are training, always start with what you know are the weakest aspects of your sailing abilities and bring them up to the level of your greatest strengths. However, the moment of truth is going to come only when you sail next to another boat, you make an adjustment, and as a result find yourself either ahead or behind that other boat. If you move ahead, look at your sail shape and see how it is different from the shape before you made the adjustment. File this new shape into your mental computer. Now you have something new you can use with confidence—until the other boat starts to sail away from you. Then go back and start working on another adjustment.

Your training program should take everything that is involved in a sailboat race, put it in a pot, melt it down, and stir hard. When you've done that long enough, you'll come out with a gold-plated program. By this I mean knowing how to set your boat up, knowing how much mast bend to put in for a given set of conditions, knowing how to trim a particular mainsail or jib—and knowing exactly what to do on the course.

When you are the skipper you must always know where you are in the boat and precisely how far you are from your bow. Knowing this distance can make the difference between establishing an overlap or missing it, or even avoiding a collision. Watch a good sailor maneuvering at a start and you will see some very exciting moves in very close quarters. But a skillful skipper is always in total control of every situation.

Think hard about all the conditions you may find, especially the water temperature, air temperature, current, projected wind strength, and sea conditions. And when it comes to your sail selection, never try to outguess Mother Nature. When you select your sail inventory, make sure the sails you choose can handle all the expected wind velocities. Never be misled by reports that there will be *only* heavy air or *only* light air. You may be badly mistaken, both on wind strength and sea conditions. So always bring sails that cover every possibility.

If you are traveling to the race site, get there in plenty of time, so you can look things over and see what the wind and sea conditions actually are. Get your charts in order, look at the projected current flows, and familiarize yourself with the geography. In short, do everything you can to prepare yourself so that you can achieve your primary prerace goal: to put your mind at ease. Try to organize things so that when you and your crew go out on the water for the first race, there are no unanswered questions about wind, current, sea conditions, and all the other factors that could have a bearing on the race.

I suppose there does come a point when you can be overprepared for a race. But in my experience this happens only when you try to get too scientific or technical about a single aspect of the racing problem. For example, you might forget about staying with the fleet and instead try to pull out something magical from the tide or wind information you have gathered. I have found it is far better to let the fleet be your guide as to where you should go. Then, if it seems reasonable, you can use whatever additional "secret" information you have developed to get just a small lead over the rest of the boats. After all, once you are in front, you can protect your lead on the second and third windward legs. You might even appear to be brilliant as you sail across the finish line well in front of everyone. But all you've really done is gotten just a small advantage from your research at the start of the race, then continued to apply it in reasoned amounts over the remainder of the course. The concept is simple enough, but lots of people forget this rule all the time.

If you are racing in a regatta, you have to think like a prize-fighter and protect yourself in the early rounds, which in sailing are the first and second windward legs. In fact, think hard about protecting yourself for the entire first race. Then, in the second race, try to do a bit more sparring. Start to test your speed with other boats, and make mental notes about their performance when you do.

I don't think it is ever smart to sail out to a corner in the first race. Instead, my strategy is to try to get a good start if the starting line is square, and for the first five minutes work hard on all the things I know are important for speed. Then I start to work on beating to the windward mark. After I have rounded the mark, I start to work on the reach, and eventually I expand my efforts to cover the entire course.

I like to finish the first race of every series knowing I have sailed well. I also like to have a good idea of what everyone else on the course is capable of, and I want to be sure I have done everything posssible to eliminate any known problems on my boat. And I try to ascertain the strengths and weaknesses of my competitors. Then I begin to build my momentum over the following races.

It's great if you can get a first-place finish in your opening race. But don't forget the most important thing to do is to sail consistently and stick to the things you know you can do well. Try to build your momentum over a series, and don't forget to match that momentum ashore by maintaining the respect of your competitors. A confident attitude is an integral part of your racing strategy, and it never should be neglected afloat or ashore.

On the water, always watch how the other crews handle themselves. This may sound funny but you can spot, almost right away, a crew that has its confidence and one that doesn't. When I sail alongside another boat I look at how the crew is sitting and how they react to another boat alongside. I see how confident they are, and this tells me who is going to be tough and who isn't. Without exception the crews that have their boathandling, their roll-tacking, and their sail shapes under control always have everything else under control as well. The reason is that they have spent enough time on the water to gain the experience, and then the confidence,

that comes from understanding the rhythm of the boat and
what it wants to tell them.

There's a picture of an ocean liner on my wall with a quote
beneath it that says "Good steering is of great value." The
quote is signed by Mr. S. Cunard, one of the founders of the
Cunard Steamship Company. Steering is certainly important,
but it goes hand-in-hand with concentration, which is the
ability to block everything else out and to focus completely on
getting your boat over the waves in harmony with the sea and
the wind. If you are sailing in close company with another
boat, it becomes even more important to concentrate and
work hard on every inch. If you can get one inch ahead of
another boat that seems to have a safe leeward on you, you
can completely reverse the situation. Now that boat has to
tack away. And that extra inch you gained can quickly become many yards, with your competitor well astern of you.

You win sailboat races by doing the best you can at all
times, of course. But what you are really doing is trying to
keep the number of your mistakes at zero. And the smallest
number of mistakes are made by those who are the best
prepared. A mistake is a frayed shroud that lets go in a race,
causing the mast to topple. A mistake is a worn batten pocket
that could easily have been taken care of before a race, but
wasn't, so the batten flies out on the first windward leg. A
mistake is not checking a deck fitting with a screwdriver to
make sure it is secure, and then finding a nut in the locked
position on the other side. A mistake is not reading the current or a windshift correctly; or lighting a cigarette just as you
come up to the starting line; or falling asleep at the start and
letting another boat come up underneath you, establish an
overlap to leeward, and take you head-to-wind. A mistake is
getting pushed off the line at the start and then kicking
yourself all around the course as you look at the stern of
everyone else's boat.

Even the best sailors commit these kinds of errors. But your
goal should be to eliminate every one of these gaffes from

your repertoire so that there is nothing between you and the finish line except the bow of your boat.

Constantly try to improve the shape of your sails and never be satisfied until they are right. When you improve your sail shape you are also going to improve your boatspeed—and that is what is going to increase your lead.

You should be thinking of ways to make your boat go faster all the time—when you are at home working on the bottom; when you sail out to the racecourse and take your wind checks; when you are starting at the proper end of the line; or when you are making sure the crew is properly involved in what is going on. It makes me happy to see lots of wrists and hands moving control lines on my boat. That movement reassures me that I am not alone. It gives me the confidence that everyone else on board wants to win the race as badly as I do.

Whenever you are in doubt about whether a particular deck layout, sail adjustment, or tactic is going to work, always look to the wind to give you your final answer. Its influence really never changes, and that may be why we so often end up with ideas that either are reworked or put into a new context. I think my good friend Rob Lansing probably is right when he says that almost everything in this sport is really a collection of old rules that are relived, or better yet, re-learned. Still, you can never afford to stop trying to do things just a little better than everyone else. Because if you do stop trying, it won't be long before someone comes sailing along—and crosses that finish line before you.

INDEX